SCOTTISH

# SCOTTISH
# INDEPENDENCE

## YES | NO

George
Kerevan

Alan
Cochrane

The
History
Press

First published 2014

The History Press
The Mill, Brimscombe Port
Stroud, Gloucestershire, GL5 2QG
www.thehistorypress.co.uk

British Library Cataloguing in Publication Data.
A catalogue record for this book is available from the British Library.

ISBN 978 0 7509 5583 6

Typesetting and origination by The History Press
Printed in Great Britain

# CONTENTS

# PART ONE

# THE CASE FOR YES

# ABOUT THE AUTHOR

George Kerevan was born in Glasgow and studied at Glasgow and Edinburgh Universities. He lectured in economics before becoming a journalist, and was Associate Editor of the *Scotsman* newspaper for nine years. His documentary films have been shown widely in America and Europe. He has served on the boards of numerous arts organisations, including the Edinburgh International Festival, Traverse Theatre, and Edinburgh Film Festival. He was an SNP candidate in the 2010 Westminster and the 2011 Scottish Parliament elections.

# PROLOGUE

On 18 September 2014, all electors in Scotland – native, English-born and resident EU citizens – will be asked to vote on the following question: 'Should Scotland be an independent country? Yes or No?' This half of our book puts forward the case on why they should vote Yes.[1]

At the very heart of the independence debate lies a deep disenchantment with the anti-democratic, over-centralised British state, and with the Oxbridge–public school elitism of its ruling London establishment. Simply put: Scotland wants independence so it can govern itself better and grow its economy free of the short-termism and casino economics of the City of London which, in the words of Business Secretary Vince Cable, are sucking the lifeblood out of the rest of the British Isles. Voting Yes is about creating the basis for a new and more harmonious partnership between the constituent nations and peoples of these British islands. Voting No is about letting the ramshackle UK state meander on from crisis to crisis.

Modern Scottish nationalism is not about flags, embassies or a romantic nineteenth-century concept of insular national sovereignty. Still less is it an expression of ethnic or racial exclusivity on the lines of right-wing nationalist movements in Eastern Europe. It is certainly not premised on anti-English feeling. The roots of the demand for Scottish self-government lie in the need to decentralise the British state, democratise British society politically and culturally, free up social mobility after a generation of stasis, and break the hold of the London city state over the culture and economy of the rest of the British Isles. Voting Yes is about creating the foundations of a twenty-first-century society that looks outwards to a globalised world rather than inwards to a Little Britain that hates Europe and lives on nostalgia for a lost imperial past.

Explaining Scottish nationalism in these terms often surprises those not privy to the debate – yet it should not. The need to reform the obsolete UK state and redefine the role of citizenship has formed the subtext of all UK politics since the Second World War. The 30-year civil war in Northern Ireland was the direct result of the failure of the British state to grant civil rights to its Catholic citizens in that province. Who gets to be a UK citizen – black, European or Muslim – has dominated politics on the doorstep since the 1950s. And the Westminster expenses scandal that exploded in 2010 is proof positive that, even in the first decade of the twenty-first century, British parliamentary structures are rotten to the core.

The vote on 18 September is about democratic reform more than the politics of identity. The main independence party is overtly proud of the fact that its initials stand for Scottish National Party, not Scottish National*ist* Party.

The SNP consciously brands its politics as an inclusive 'civic nationalism' in opposition to the xenophobic 'ethnic nationalism' that scars much of Europe. Officially, the party describes its ideology as social democratic on the Nordic model and most members take a dim view of neo-liberal economics. Unlike the wave of populist and self-styled nationalist movements now besetting Scandinavia and Eastern Europe, the SNP is fervently committed to EU membership and opening Scotland to inward migration.

The SNP's disparagers dismiss the party's vision either as 'independence lite', or accuse Alex Salmond (Scotland's First Minister and leader of the SNP) of offering a deliberately disingenuous vision of self-government in order to win over sceptical voters. Neither is true. The leaders of the No campaign fail to appreciate that the SNP's project is not the traditional nineteenth-century model of state autonomy but the rebalancing of political and economic relationships within the British Isles in order to meet the challenges of the twenty-first century. In Salmond's vision, an independent Scotland and the rest of the United Kingdom (which we will call rUK for short) will share a common Head of State, a common currency, free trade, and a common security strategy through NATO. Salmond is offering a new British confederation in everything but name. In this *de facto* confederation, the individual nations of the British Isles would have their own parliaments and domestic tax arrangements, meaning (crucially) that the people of England regain their direct political voice. An English Parliament would assuage English populism and let traditional English liberal values shine. The peoples of the Atlantic Archipelago will be free to look outward to Europe and the world, rather than inward as a parochial Little Britain.

Unfortunately for the entire people of these islands, the big three Westminster parties are unwilling to think strategically about reforming British state structures, far less accept Salmond's elegant solution. On the contrary, Labour, Tories and Lib Dems united to veto allowing Scottish voters a second option on the 18 September ballot – that of devolving more powers to the Scottish Parliament over taxes and welfare. Repeated polls suggest such 'devo max' would command an overwhelming majority yet the Westminster big three prefer attempting to shoot the SNP political fox rather than advancing their own (or any) vision of reform within the UK as presently constituted. But then, throughout the postwar period, Westminster has systematically delayed every reform of the British state until it was dragged kicking and screaming to accept change. In the 1979 Scottish referendum, a majority voted for creating a Parliament in Edinburgh (then called an Assembly) by 1,239,937 votes to 1,153,500. But Westminster had the arrogance to set aside the result on the spurious grounds that it was insufficient indication of the popular will – perhaps the most disgraceful flouting of democracy in a Western European state in the past 50 years.

But there is far more to the 18 September referendum than tinkering with the pieces on the British constitutional chessboard. The Scottish political philosopher Tom Nairn aptly sums up the moment:

Scotland, Wales and Northern Ireland are not attempting old-style nation-statehood: they are (and indeed, can't help being) in search of a new mode of distinctive development – post-globalisation self-rule, liberated from the contortions of imperialism and warfare, and adapted to circumstances in which the scale of statehood is no longer so important.

In seeking independence, the Scots are not trying to redefine Britishness *per se*. They are trying to define *sui generus* new ways of living and governing for the twenty-first century – a century which will have to accommodate the rise of Asia, mass global migration, climate change, and permanent cultural revolution stimulated by biotechnology and the invasion of every corner of human life by the Internet. A Yes vote on 18 September is as much about redefining the future as repairing the past. It is about building a new Scottish nation state with the institutions to meet these profound challenges. In the following pages we will explore in more detail not only the arguments for Scottish independence but also the sort of new community the Scots are seeking to build. This is more a revolution than a referendum.

<hr>

*Notes*

1   The independence debate is awash in a sea of statistics. In order to make the following essay palatable, I have avoided some of the more technical issues. Readers are directed to 'Scotland's Future', the fulsome 650-page White Paper available on the Scottish Government's website.

# 1

# THE BETTER GOVERNANCE ARGUMENT

## *Britain Isn't Working*

The first argument for voting Yes is basic: Scotland is a distinct community best governed from Edinburgh, not from 400 miles away. Once upon a time, technology and education limited the ability of small communities to deal directly with the world. Intermediaries in the form of centralised states and empires acted as bridges to the rest of the globe. Today, in the age of the Internet, such political interlocutors are unnecessary and even a barrier to national self-expression. Scots feel increasingly alienated from the dysfunctional British state and from British identity itself. Contemporary Britain has failed to forge a new national identity for the post-imperial era – resisting democratic reforms till the last minute, while lapsing into cultural nostalgia and sometimes Little Englander racism. Worse, despite the trappings of liberal democracy, Britain has evolved into a thoroughgoing oligarchy based in London, run by a privately educated elite on behalf of the super rich.

In an opinion poll for the *Sunday Times* in late 2013, Scots were asked: 'Imagine yourself meeting someone from overseas for the first time. Regardless of how you plan to vote in the referendum, would you feel more proud introducing yourself as Scottish or British?' Some 63 per cent answered Scottish and only 19 per cent British. Consistently since 1999, in 'forced choice' polls between Scottishness and Britishness, the proportion opting for British identity has never bested 20 per cent. The numbers doubting their Britishness are far higher than the numbers supporting political independence. This is a new social phenomenon that has arisen since the 1950s with the collapse of the British Empire. Whatever happens in the 18 September referendum, it is clear that a significant majority of Scots – starting with the post-war baby boomers – has grown doubtful of their Britishness.

Disenchantment with British institutions is not limited to Scotland (though the rise of Scottish nationalism provides a political way of resolving such discontent north of the border). The 2009 British Social Attitudes survey indicates that 40 per cent of the UK public 'almost never' trust 'national government'. This compares to only 10 per cent in 1974. While growing distrust of governments is an international phenomenon, the UK tops the European league table for the decline in faith in parliamentary institutions, showing a massive 30 point fall in the percentage of people saying they 'tend to trust parliament' since 1997. Only a miserly 19 per cent now say they trust Westminster. The growing distrust of national government and parliamentary institutions in the UK also extends to the main Westminster political parties, with barely 12 per cent of British citizens saying they 'tend to trust' mainstream party organisations. There has been a corresponding decline in public confidence in other UK institutions since the 1980s, including the police, justice system, BBC and even the armed forces. This mood of political detachment has translated into a rise in extra-parliamentary social protest. Survey data shows that the proportion of the British adult population engaging in 'lawful demonstrations' has doubled from around 8 per cent in the 1970s (a turbulent decade) to 16 per cent in the first millennium of the new century.

To understand this existential crisis of Britishness we need to appreciate the forces that created the present archaic British state and why that historical glue has come unstuck in the era of globalisation. Simply put: the contemporary British state system was invented in a pre-industrial era, was honed for running a colonial empire that no longer exists, and has never been modernised in its working essentials since the late seventeenth century. The result is an over-centralised, elitist political superstructure that is not fit for purpose in the era of YouTube and Twitter. It is a political structure dominated by Metropolitan vested interests and so uniquely incapable of adequate domestic reform – hence the requirement for Scottish independence.

The British state is a product of the English Civil War, which (despite its religious ideological guise) was a nascent bourgeois political revolution that pitted yeoman capitalist farmers and City trading interests against the Absolute Monarchy and its feudal aristocracy. This civil war exhausted both sides and led to an historic political compromise between aristocratic landowners and early mercantile capitalists. As a result, the British constitutional model is neither feudal nor democratic, but a horrible compromise between the two. It remains uniquely archaic, authoritarian and centralist, yet with enough democratic trappings (extracted at great cost) to provide a cultural fig leaf for its ancient lineage. The absolutism of the old feudal monarchy has been translated bodily into the doctrine of the sovereignty (dictatorship) of the Westminster parliament. This comes surrounded with semi-feudal hereditary trappings that include an appointed House of Lords to act as a guard against populist legislation passed by (God forbid!) elected representatives. Parliament rules in the interest of the City of London and an Oxbridge-educated establishment, with very few checks and balances. Ordinary Britons remain legally the subjects of the Crown (i.e. of the Parliamentary dictatorship) rather than free citizens in whom sovereignty is vested. Hereditary or appointed institutions remain impervious to democratic accountability, from the BBC to the Head of State, even if the Windsor family has consciously adopted the trappings of a middle-class family in this age of faux 'reality' television.

Social mobility in this archaic Britain – after a brief thaw caused by the necessity of fighting two, technology-dominated wars – has frozen. In fact, 'modern' Britain has one of the lowest rates of social mobility in the developed world. Data from the OECD think tank show that earnings in the UK are more likely to reflect the father's income bracket than in any other industrial nation. The proportion of university undergraduates from the poorest family backgrounds has dropped precipitously since the 1970s. In the Britain of

2012, 32 per cent of MPs, 51 per cent of senior medical con-
sultants, 54 per cent of FTSE-100 chief execs, 54 per cent of
top journalists, and 70 per cent of High Court judges went
to private schools, though only 7 per cent of the UK population attended them. The top 1 per cent of the Britons owns
a greater share of national income than at any time since the
1930s. This plutocracy dominates government: more than
half of the Cabinet elected in 2010, including David Cameron,
the Prime Minister; George Osborne, the Chancellor; and
Nick Clegg, the Lib Dem Deputy Prime Minister, went to private schools and were independently wealthy.

The United Kingdom as presently constituted is a political
system built to serve vested interests. It has been this way
since the seventeenth century, yielding to new social and
economic forces only with the stiffest of resistance. Today,
it has evolved into what Ferdinand Mount, former head of
Margaret Thatcher's policy unit, has termed 'a very British oligarchy'.[1] With real incomes for the majority of the population
now decaying, and with limited prospects for social advance-
ment among the young, it is little wonder the mass of the
British population has grown disenchanted with this obsolete
system. No wonder many Scots want to leave it.

## The Invention of Britishness

Why is the British state suffering this (terminal) crisis of
legitimacy at the start of the twenty-first century, rather
than before? Nations and their concomitant mass identities
are political constructs, especially in the modern capitalist

era. The most respected theorists of this process of state-building are Ernest Gellner, the British-Czech philosopher, and Benedict Anderson, a polyglot British-Irish-American academic.[2] The core argument advanced by Gellner and Anderson is that national allegiance is invented as a mobilising force to aid 'modernisation', i.e. the creation of a capitalist market economy and subsequent industrialisation. Modernisation requires the creation of an enabling state led by a rising bourgeoisie. An invented nationality is necessary to mobilise popular support for the new state against internal and external enemies, and against old allegiances – feudal, religious, or political. A complicit intelligentsia plays a crucial role in forming and disseminating the national myths that create allegiance to this new state.

But Britain never went through a true 'modernising' process to update its state machinery and 'national' cultural cement in order to facilitate capitalist development. Here lie the roots of the present constitutional crisis. Britain got stuck with the job half done. Other nations had revolutions, colonial rebellion and war in order to sweep away the old, pre-capitalist regimes and create (and re-create) modern entities; e.g. the USA, France, Japan and Germany. Such modern states are not necessarily democratic or liberal, but – as in the case of post-Maoist China – they command popular allegiance for the modernising 'project'. However, democratic institutions remain central to the most successful capitalist states as they facilitate a compliant labour force, prevent political vested interests from interfering with private property, and encourage the meritocracy needed to foster continuing entrepreneurial and technological breakthroughs. On the contrary, Britain's semi-democracy, centralising and elitist institutions, and (accidental) avoidance of domestic revolution, have all contrived to produce social and economic stasis. The archaic British regime was good at garnering imperial plunder and winning wars – the reason for its longevity. It is not good at mobilising the population for economic renewal in the era of globalisation because the latter is premised on social mobility and constantly revolutionising the ownership of capital. Hence the current crisis.

True, Britain's early industrial revolution was seminal. Yet it was pioneered in Scotland and the North of England – outside the London elite. Protected by closed imperial markets, and subordinate to the financial and merchant class in the City of London, British manufacturing was quickly overtaken by rising new industrial powers in America and Germany. Down to the 1960s, British manufacturing remained dominated by under-capitalised, medium-scale family firms that lagged far behind America and Germany in mass production techniques. With the loss of Empire and bankrupted by the Second World War, the British economy faced disaster. It was rescued by the accidental discovery of North Sea oil (which paid the import bills) and the resurgence of the City of London as an offshore banking centre facilitated by Mrs Thatcher and later New Labour. The old manufacturing and mining periphery in Scotland and the English North – ever a den of political resistance to London – was left to de-industrialise in favour of 'financial services' concentrated in the South East. In the 1990s, City financial donors effectively bought the Labour Party; in return, Tony Blair and Gordon Brown collaborated in the destruction of post-war shareholder capitalism and its replacement by a system of debt finance. Result:

the Credit Crunch of 2008 and the worst loss of output in the British economy since the 1930s.

If the archaic British system retarded and distorted capitalist modernisation, why did it last so long? One reason was that it evolved a modicum of popular support – but it is precisely this support that has evaporated. The most cited text on British national identity is *Britons: Forging the Nation 1707–1837*, written by academic Linda Colley.[3] Gordon Brown was so taken with Colley's analysis that he awarded her a CBE. Colley's thesis is that Britishness as a new mass identity was invented during the 150 years immediately after the Act of Union in 1707, overlaying but definitely not eliminating English, Scottish and Welsh identities – she tends to ignore Ireland. The cement for this new Britishness was provided by three factors: a common Protestantism that reinforced a sense of 'British exceptionalism'; the first use of a modern popular mobilisation against exterior enemies (France) which encouraged the masses to feel they had a stake in the new state; and the creation of a 'middle class' monarchy by the Hanoverians, which engendered a sense of allegiance. Colley concludes with a truism: '… the factors that provided for the forging of a British nation in the past have largely ceased to operate'. Protestantism has been replaced by secularism; the Windsor monarchy has stuttered from crisis to crisis; the Empire is gone; and it is two generations since the Second World War and the last collective mobilisation against an external enemy. Cue the end of Britishness with the demise of the Second World War generation.

Why did Scots buy into Britishness to begin with? For a long time leading Scots showed uncritical enthusiasm for

English institutions, liberties and values, to the point even of wanting Scottish civil society anglicised. But this North Britishness should not be read as the emergence of a 'pan-Britannic national identity'. It was actually the result of an emergent Scottish bourgeoisie believing an English-style political order and English bourgeois values were central to modernising 'backward', feudal Scotland. This process fits well with Benedict Anderson's view of nationalism as a modernising ideology. It also explains the marked absence of a classic romantic nationalist myth about ancient, pre-Union Scotland, despite the best efforts of Sir Walter Scott's novels. North Britons (and they still exist today in the Scottish Labour and Tory parties) see the institutions and liberal values of the Anglo-British state as a guarantee against an alleged Scottish 'parochialism'. Unfortunately, it was the Anglo-British state that turned out to be archaic and anti-modern.

The Scots aristocrats who originally signed the Treaty of Union because they thought it would guarantee their remaining feudal rights found those privileges revoked by Westminster after 1745, in a predictable move towards political centralisation following the failed Jacobite rising. Scots served as the administrative and entrepreneurial shock troops of the Empire but they were never allowed into the inner sanctum of the Anglo-British state machine in any numbers. So in the late nineteenth century, an increasingly frustrated 'North British' industrial bourgeoisie began to agitate for administrative devolution to Edinburgh, leading to the creation of the Scottish Office in 1885. Home Rule Bills were actually passed at Westminster in 1913 and 1914, with the intention of giving Scotland Dominion status equivalent to Australia and Canada, but the reform was sidelined at the outbreak of the First World War. Intensified international competition after the Great War forced the Scottish industrial bourgeoisie to seek state protection, which paradoxically reinforced their support for the Union. Their final reward was nationalisation and external takeover that eliminated them as a social entity by the end of the 1960s. So ended the main social prop for Unionism in Scotland, along with the decline of the Protestant Ascendancy. At the precise same historical moment (during the first wave of de-industrialisation that saw off the great Clyde shipyards) working-class Scots and the local intelligentsia began losing faith in being North British, and re-embraced Scottish nationalism as a 'modernising' project.

## Objection 1: A New Britishness is Possible

Is a new Britishness possible given the collapse of the institutional foundations that created it in the first place? In a *Guardian* article in 2006 Linda Colley admitted that there are now 'many people in the UK who do not consider themselves British'. However, her solutions were trivial: teaching a standardised history of Britain in the 'national curriculum' (she seems ignorant that the Scottish and English education systems are separate), a new Bill of Citizen Rights, plus 'a new language of citizenship' – whatever that is.

The most interesting figure to grapple with a post-imperial definition of Britishness is Gordon Brown, though with equally vacuous results. Brown explicitly abandons Linda

Colley's institutional basis for national identity (Protestantism, monarchy, Empire) and replaces it with the notion of ageless 'shared values' that supposedly define Britishness. Reversing Colley's causation, Brown says these values actually shaped British institutions. And what are these transcendental core values? He argues, with a straight face: 'being creative, adaptable and outward-looking, believing in liberty, duty and fair play'. But it is idealist nonsense to suggest that values (as in behavioural paradigms) are encoded in particular cultures over millennia, remaining independent of the economic, class and political organisation of those communities. Also, Brown's choice of 'shared' British values are anodyne, politically safe, and found in many other cultures. In what way is creativity unique to Britain, for instance? However, it is interesting that the notions of duty and fair play are classic ideals espoused by English intellectuals and taught in English public schools.

That said, Brown's project is entirely understandable – trying to define a new political identity for a decaying Anglo-British state which is increasingly multi-ethnic and multicultural; where London has become virtually an autonomous global city; and where the devolved regions are increasingly going their own way. The London-based *Economist* magazine, commenting on the prospect of a Yes vote in the independence referendum, has opined that such a new 'modern' Britishness has already begun to emerge since the 1990s – a shift it thinks will lead Scotland to reject separation. It refers to the emergence of a classless, common lifestyle, itself the result of mass consumerism and modern technology. But the ubiquity of the Western consumer model and its values across the globe has hardly eroded national identity – witness China or Brazil.

In fact, Britishness has entered a new stage of disintegration. The ruling elite has steadfastly ignored rising English popular discontent, as exhibited in a growing opposition to membership of the EU, worries about multiculturalism, and complaints about alleged special treatment for the devolved regions. The meltdown of the euro will, at some stage, lead to an 'in-out' referendum in Britain. That could see the UK leave the EU and fracture the Tory Party – creating the conditions for a new political expression of English national identity. Meanwhile, a quarter century of civil war in Northern Ireland (one side-effect of the decline of Protestantism) has ended in a temporary truce in which the Irish nationalists have, effectively, seized control of the local state machine. It is interesting that all those trying to imagine a new form of pan-British identity, especially Gordon Brown, never include Northern Ireland.

Others on the Labour left claim that Britishness has already been redefined around post-war social democratic values (specifically the NHS) and that the Union now exists to defend this consensus from the Tories. But this post-war version of Britishness as a social democratic 'New Jerusalem' is itself threatened by economic crisis and the rise of New Labour ideas on welfare 'targeting'. In fact, it is the SNP that has retained a genuine social democratic vision and only a Yes vote will guarantee its implementation north of the border. Incidentally, attempts by Labour Unionists to make the NHS the heart of Britishness forget one thing: the first state-funded, universal health service in the British Isles was not the NHS, but the Highlands and Islands Medical Service, set up by the Scottish Office in 1913 under a Liberal government. Had the Second World War not intervened, that service would have been extended to the Lowlands. As it was, by 1939, a prototype free, state medical service was available in Glasgow. All this was supported – indeed driven – by the Scottish medical community. When the NHS came into being in 1948, it was embraced by doctors north of the border. But in England, the BMA, the doctors' union, fought state medicine tooth and nail.

Paradoxically, it is the SNP that is proposing a new cultural and institutional basis for modern 'Britishness', based on progressive values, revived social mobility and a historic break with London's grip on power. The SNP wants not only a *de facto* confederation of the British Isles but also what Alex Salmond has christened a 'social union' between Scotland and England. As Salmond explains it, this social union will operate at the personal level, given the intermarriage and common bonds between people in all the different nations of the British Isles. It will find expression in the revival of strong civil society throughout these islands, on the model that Scotland (in the absence of its own parliament) developed after 1707. It is also unthinkable that after Scottish independence, Westminster can go on as before. Inevitably, a Yes vote will lead to calls for devolved parliaments in England and more powers for Cardiff and Stormont. A strengthened social union, plus the invigorating effects of equal participation in decision-making by the other nations and regions, will constitute the first true 'modernising' revolution in the British Isles.

1   Ferdinand Mount is perhaps the most respected and influential Tory ideologue of the past generation. When he denounces the corruption of the system, the game is up. See his *The New Few* (London 2012)

2   See especially Anderson's *Imagined Communities: Reflections on the Origin and Spread of Nationalism* (London, 1983)

3   Linda Colley, *Britons: Forging the Nation 1707–1837* (London, 1993)

# 2

# THE ECONOMIC ARGUMENT

## *Independence Means Faster Growth for Scotland*

The No campaign contends that Scotland is the richer for being part of the United Kingdom. But over the 30-year period from 1976 to 2006, the average rate of growth in the UK was 2.3 per cent yet only 1.8 per cent in Scotland. That means growth north of the border – for an entire historical period – was one fifth less than the UK. This is hardly an indicator that Scotland is 'better together' in the Union. A Yes vote is necessary for Scotland to recover its capacity for economic growth.

How have other comparable independent European economies performed? The answer is much better. According to OECD data, in the 30-year period 1977 to 2007, Scotland's average GDP growth rate was 1.9 per cent. This was bettered by Ireland (5.4), Iceland (3.4), Norway (3.1), Finland (2.9), Austria (2.4), and Sweden (2.3). The average annual growth rate for those six nations combined is 3.35 per cent – nearly 60 per cent better than the Scottish performance. Five of these six did not have the benefit of oil.

Why has the Scottish economy fared so badly inside the Union especially after the Second World War? There are three main reasons, all of which have their roots in decisions made in London and which Scotland was powerless to prevent. They are: post-war nationalisation of Scottish heavy industry and the transfer of managerial control to London; subsequent deliberate de-industrialisation in Scotland caused by London-centred control, short-term investment decisions by the City and the high-value petro pound; finally, the massive population loss caused through emigration, as a result of de-industrialisation.

The key explanation for Scotland's economic decline lies in the destruction of local business ownership following the enforced nationalisation of Scottish industry by Westminster governments after the Second World War, with the subsequent transfer of corporate HQs to London. Among the industries affected were coal, steel, shipbuilding, road haulage, and airlines. Post-war plans by Prestwick-based Scottish Airlines – then one of the biggest private airlines in the world – to create a global passenger network were shattered when its scheduled routes were handed over to new, Heathrow-based nationalised services. Calls by Scottish MPs and chambers of commerce to have local control of public industries devolved to Edinburgh were rejected. The 1950s and 1960s did see new industries such as car manufacturing parachuted into Scotland temporarily using subsidies. But turning Scotland into a branch plant economy merely intensified the destruction of local enterprise and these firms disappeared when the subsidies came to an end under Margaret Thatcher. With its industrial base and manufacturing class undermined, Scotland inside the Union was doomed thereafter to slow economic growth.

The accident of North Sea oil arrived in time to pay for UK imports for another generation, but true to the short-term thinking inculcated by the City and Westminster, this windfall was wasted on consumption rather than invested, as in Norway. The North Sea bonanza had one lasting effect: it allowed Maggie Thatcher to slash tax rates and give Britain the outward semblance of a boom economy by deregulating the banks and pumping out credit. The City of London came to dominate the UK economy and economic policy, while Scotland's manufacturing base shrank. Thatcher was also happy to see Britain's newfound oil wealth push up the value of sterling, curbing inflation and attracting global funds to London. A strong pound brought de-industrialisation in its wake, as Scotland's traditional export industries lost competitiveness.

Nothing changed when New Labour arrived in office in 1997. Gordon Brown continued to favour the City bubble economy over manufacturing in Scotland and the north of England. The result was a banking meltdown in 2008. In 1997, the year Brown became Chancellor, the index of industrial production in the UK was 99.7. Ten years later, in 2007, the high point before the financial collapse, industrial output stood only at 100.3. In other words, during the decade that Brown presided over the UK economy, output in manufacturing and energy industries flatlined. This was not fate. In the same decade, German manufacturing output went up by an average of 2.9 per cent every year. Swedish factory output went up by a stunning 5.8 per cent per every year – proof that a small industrial economy could prosper.

The decimation of Scotland's native entrepreneurial class led to a morbidly low new business birth rate, limited research and development expenditure and a notoriously poor innovation rate. Emigration robbed Scotland not only of skilled labour but management talent. Unionist economists such as Professor Brian Ashcroft, of the Fraser of Allander Institute, claim these economic weaknesses have nothing to do with constitutional issues but somehow represent innate Scottish failure. On the contrary, they have everything to do with the lack of economic decision-making powers in Scotland and the growing dominance of the City in determining UK economic policy. Ask yourself: would an independent Scotland in the 1970s have squandered its oil revenues, handed over its oil industry to foreign ownership, and deliberately engineered a high-value currency that was bound to kill off its native engineering export industry? If the answers are no, then the constitutional question lies at the heart of the economic growth debate.

Pro-Union economists like Professor Ashcroft use a special argument to ignore poor Scottish economic growth. They say it is wrong to concentrate on overall national GDP growth – the size of the economic cake as a whole. Instead, they argue one should look at economic growth per capita, which reflects the standard of living, or share of the cake going to individuals. On this measure, the gap between Scotland and the UK is much narrower, with individual Scottish living standards staying close to the UK average over the past generation and occasionally even surpassing it. However, the reason for this has nothing to do with the Union being good for Scots. Scotland's seeming ability to maintain its share (per head) of the UK cake is the result of the massive population loss that resulted from industrial decline. In the heyday of Scottish industrialisation, 1855 to 1900, the Scottish population grew from 2.98 million to 4.44 million, or 49 per cent. The population of Glasgow virtually doubled in the 1890s and turn of the century as immigrants flooded in from Ireland, the Highlands and Europe. Thereafter, economic depression resulted in a mass emigration. Between 1921 and 1951, there was a net loss of 610,000 people – over 10 per cent of the entire population. Another net loss of 600,000 Scots occurred between 1951 and 1971. This exodus drained the entrepreneurial lifeblood from Clydeside and industrial towns such as Dundee. Paradoxically, population loss meant that Scotland's modest rate of economic growth kept standards of living advancing – there were fewer people to share the cake. Scotland's population today, despite a rise since devolution, is barely 1 per cent higher than in the early 1950s. Contrast that with Ireland, which saw an increase in population of over 40 per cent by reversing outmigration (at least until the current downturn). You cannot drive hundreds of thousands of Scots abroad and then claim the Union delivered per capita growth at home.

## After Independence: The Economic Big Bang

Can the low growth of the last 30 years be reversed through voting Yes? What exactly would change? What would a

Scottish nation state be able to do to help business and the economy that – given enough fiscal devolution – couldn't be done inside the United Kingdom? Put more succinctly: what economic 'big bang' does independence provide over fiscal devolution? It's a fair point. The answer comes in four parts: a more efficient tax system; increased social mobility; a welcome for inward migration; and a boost to investment.

### (1) A more efficient tax system

Where an independent Scotland gains, even keeping sterling as its currency, is in having the ability to create a new taxation system tailored to local needs – essentially one that helps the economy to grow. The current UK system of taxation is a bureaucratic mess that is unfit for purpose. Devolving fiscal autonomy to Scotland inside the UK might let a Scottish government vary tax rates but principally it would not give Holyrood the scope to rewrite the tax code – that only comes with independence.

This is the main argument in a series of papers published by the respected Institute of Fiscal Studies in late 2013.[1] The IFS findings were reported by the No campaign as proving an independent Scotland would have to raise taxes if it wanted to maintain current levels of public spending as the population ages. Actually, such a fiscal gap holds true for Scotland inside or outside the UK, and for the UK itself. Income tax is being devolved to Holyrood in 2016 anyway, whoever runs Scotland will have to cope with that. However – and here is what the No campaign deliberately ignored – the IFS pointed out that only an independent Scotland was in a position to refashion the overall tax structure to promote economic growth and so raise the necessary cash to fill any so-called fiscal 'black holes'.

According to the IFS:

> ... the current system of income taxes and welfare benefits creates serious disincentives to work for many with relatively low potential earning power ... Scottish independence would provide an opportunity to make sensible changes to the tax system in Scotland that successive UK governments have failed to make ... the creation of a new state is surely the best opportunity that is ever likely to present itself for radical and rational tax reform, starting from first principles, which has the potential to unlock really significant economic benefits.

The IFS recommends a number of ways the tax system could be reformed to boost Scottish investment and productivity, and hence growth. Chief among these is the introduction of an allowance for corporate equity, or ACE. This is an allowance for the opportunity cost of equity finance similar to the deduction already given for the costs of debt finance (i.e. interest payments). Introducing an ACE in an independent Scotland would make it a more attractive location for mobile investments that were equity-financed. Private equity firms would be especially interested. An ACE would also provide an incentive for companies operating in both Scotland and rUK to use more equity finance in Scotland and more debt finance in rUK, since debt interest would be deductible in either country. Note: equity finance is more likely to remain in a company long term and to encourage savers in Scotland to invest in local business enterprise, raising productivity.

Incidentally, the IFS suggests that independent Scotland, with an aging population, will have to find the equivalent of an extra 1.9 per cent of GDP to fund future public spending levels. However, it calculates this by assuming Scottish economic growth will be an average of 2 per cent per annum until around 2060 (i.e. much as it has been for the past 30 years). But if growth in an independent Scotland were anywhere near the levels of other small European industrial economies in the last generation – which were considerably higher than either Scotland or the UK – the fiscal gap posited by the IFS disappears.

*(2) Increased social mobility adds to entrepreneurship*
At one stroke, independence will break the organic link with the London-based elites who have frozen Britain and Scotland into social immobility. New social opportunities born of creating a modern nation state will loosen attitudes to change and create a fertile cultural climate for innovation and entrepreneurship in the decade after a Yes vote.

Changing patterns of social mobility are due primarily to changes in the occupational structure – to changes in the availability of places at the top of the social class ladder. This explains why British social mobility was plastic during the decades immediately after the Second World War, when the expansion of technical, professional and semi-professional employment allied to the contraction of manual occupations opened up new opportunities for people from lower social classes to enter the middle class. But in the past three decades, social mobility in the UK has been blocked by the stranglehold over the remaining senior professional jobs held by the private school and Oxbridge-educated elite concentrated in London. Independence will remove this exclusive social network and, by increasing economic growth, open up the Scottish labour market to new forces. This, in turn, will have a demonstrative, positive impact on the morale of young Scots, increasing ambition and drive. These latter impacts are difficult to quantify but a 2010 study done by the Boston Consulting Group for the Sutton Trust estimated that encouraging UK school underachievers to reach average secondary attainment and subsequent employment would add around 4 percentage points to GDP. A similar impact would seem likely for an independent Scotland. Note also that independence will require domestic replacement for administrative and managerial posts presently filled in London – thus expanding the Scottish professional labour market. This is broadly revenue neutral to the new Scottish exchequer as Scots taxpayers already fund these posts pro rata inside the UK set-up.

### (3) Instant welcome to migrants boosts economic growth

An independent Scotland would have more liberal immigration rules than the UK, instantly improving labour market performance. A points-based immigration system would be introduced to actually increase the number of skilled immigrants coming to work in Scotland from outside the EU – just as Westminster is restricting such immigration into the UK. Independent Scotland would also reintroduce the student visas removed by Westminster.

The economic benefits of inward migration are as concrete as those of inward capital investment. Fresh human capital brings skills, offsets an aging domestic population, makes labour markets more flexible, and adds to the entrepreneurial pool. Yet the direction of Westminster governments (and much of social attitudes south of the border) is to oppose future immigration to the point of being racist. In Scotland, on the contrary, the SNP Government has sought powers to attract more foreign workers and students. After independence, Scotland would be free to set its own immigration policy in order to encourage economic growth. Boosting Scotland's working population is vital in this regard. In 2011/12, Scotland attracted 45,116 migrants from the rest of the UK and 35,900 from overseas. However, in the same period, 42,078 Scots migrated to elsewhere in the UK and 26,200 left for a foreign country. This meant there was a net inward migration of only 12,738 to balance the leavers, most of whom were well-qualified, younger Scots.

The economics of Scottish demography are clear. Scotland's population is predicted to grow by only 4.4 per cent by 2062 compared to 22.8 per cent for the UK, thanks to lower birth rates, shorter life expectancy and lower immigration. This explains the so-called fiscal gap identified by the IFS. Yet if Scotland can raise its population growth, GDP growth jumps. An extra 5,000 net increase per annum to the population from inward migrating workers would add around 1 percentage point to annual GDP, inside a decade. Make that 10,000 and the fiscal gap of 1.9 per cent identified by the IFS disappears (though this is additional taxable output rather than new public revenue *per se*). A final point: is there room for more immigrants? Yes: the percentage of people not born in Britain living in Scotland is significantly lower than for the UK as a whole: 6.6 per cent compared to some 12 per cent.

## (4) Investment to re-industrialise

The SNP Government plans a major boost to capital investment spending after independence, reversing the situation under Westminster tutelage. Ambitiously, it calls this strategy 'the reindustrialisation of Scotland'.

Historically, the UK (with its nations and regions) has lagged well behind other developed economies in terms of its overall rates of capital investment, both public and private. This investment is crucial to boosting productivity and competitiveness. The CIA World Factbook ranks the UK an astonishing 137 out of 150 countries for gross fixed investment as a percentage of GDP. The UK's total fixed capital investment – including housing – is actually the lowest of any country in Western Europe, according to an Economist Intelligence Unit report ('Upgrading Britain', 2011). The UK's fixed investment as a percentage of GDP between 1980 and 2009 averaged only 17.4 per cent – with a lot of that going into the housing bubble in later years. This compares with an average of 21 per cent in fifteen major European economies. Among the smaller industrial economies similar in population to Scotland, investment to GDP ratio was: Switzerland (24.1), Austria (22.7), Norway (22.3) and Finland (22.0). If anything, matters have deteriorated since the economic crisis of 2008. Increasing Scotland's capital investment ratio to the European average would put an extra £5 billion per annum into boosting productivity. Benchmarking the small, high-flyer economies would see annual investment jump by around £7.7 billion. How can this be achieved quickly? An independent Scotland will control its own fiscal levers. The aim is not to raise public borrowing but rather to shift fiscal incentives (as with the ACE equity allowance discussed above) to promote corporate investment and R&D spending.

Much of the debate on tax incentives revolves erroneously around inward investment. Actually Scotland is a capital-rich nation with a sophisticated banking system. What is required is a domestic bank regulatory and fiscal regime that promotes long-term capital lending for domestic firms. One option afforded by independence would be a publicly-owned industrial and infrastructure investment bank operated on commercial principles, but able to tap international capital markets. The Scottish Government has already created a limited prototype in the shape of the Scottish Investment Bank. Nevertheless, the SNP also proposes to cut corporation tax to enlarge the pool of local and foreign capital investment.

## Conclusion

Independence will certainly entail economic risk. But economic risk is endemic in a global free market, inside the Union or out of it. The Scotland we live in – with its youth unemployment, decaying high streets, universities reduced to corporate affiliates, and poverty in the midst of plenty – is not the Scotland most people desire. Greater devolution will not cure Scotland's ills or give youth a future. To do that, Scots must take economic power and resources into their own hands. If they fail, they are no worse off than under

David Cameron's austerity plan. If they succeed, they can give Scotland's young people hope and old folk greater security.

*Notes*

1   'Taxing an independent Scotland' by Stuart Adam, Paul Johnson and Barra Roantree. Institute for Fiscal Studies, October 2013. See also 'Fiscal Sustainability of an Independent Scotland' by Michael Amior, Rowena Crawford and Gemma Tetlow, Institute of Fiscal Studies, November 2013. IFS publications can be found on the Institute's website.

# 3

# ECONOMIC OBJECTIONS TO INDEPENDENCE ANSWERED

## 1. What if rUK Says No to a Currency Union?

The No campaign has made the currency issue its leading area of attack. Speaking in Edinburgh on 13 February 2014, Chancellor George Osborne explicitly ruled out a currency union on the grounds it 'would not be in the interests of either the people of Scotland or the remaining UK'. In a coordinated response from the No camp, Osborne's pre-vote diktat was echoed by Labour Shadow Chancellor Ed Balls and Lib Dem Treasury Secretary Danny Alexander. However, the SNP position remains that retaining the sterling link is in the interests of both Scotland and the rUK and that Osborne is bluffing in order to diminish the Yes vote in the referendum. Regardless, the SNP intends to maintain the use of sterling after a Yes victory, and maintains the Treasury will be forced by circumstance to negotiate with Edinburgh over joint management of the currency.

Why is the SNP set on keeping sterling? It is the simplest option during the constitutional transition. All Scotland's prices, pensions, investment projects, debts and savings are calculated and valued in sterling. Changing that would cause uncertainty, disrupt business, create a situation where price conversions could be fiddled, and add to business costs. But keeping sterling has costs: Scotland will continue to have the same interest rates as the rUK. Traditionally, interest rates have been higher in the UK than the rest of Europe in order to fight inflation generated by the over-heated economy of the English South East. That hurt Scottish businesses and wallets. Keeping the pound also means Scotland has no control over the external exchange rate. If the pound goes up in value against foreign currencies like the dollar, Scottish exports will be hurt. However, Scotland inside the UK currently has to live with interest rates and the exchange rate set by the Bank of England. In that sense, keeping sterling after independence makes Scotland no worse off. Where a proper currency union trumps the current set-up is that it would involve Scottish representation on the Bank of England's Monetary Policy Committee, which sets interest rates. This will ensure interest rates take into account Scottish needs. Such representation is hardly novel – the US Federal Reserve and the Bank of Canada both have regional representatives on their leading bodies as a matter of course.

What happens if Westminster opposes a common sterling area? The answer is Scotland will go on using sterling the day after independence because that is what it uses already. Prices, savings, benefits and pensions would still be priced in pounds. Banks would still lend in pounds – most monetary transfers are electronic and by definition don't use paper notes printed by the Bank of England. Westminster would have no power to ban a sovereign nation from using sterling, which is a freely tradable currency on global markets. In fact, just such an informal sterling currency zone already exists between mainland Britain and the Channel Islands (Jersey and Guernsey) and the Isle of Man – which formally are not part of either the UK or EU. The UK Treasury lives with this situation even though these islands have extensive offshore banking sectors with multibillion sterling liabilities far in excess of their modest GDPs.

Two issues would arise from keeping sterling without negotiating arrangements for a formal currency zone. First: Scotland would have no direct say in the determination of the base interest rate by the Bank of England. However, in the immediate future (say the next 5 years) this is of modest importance as rates are likely to stay at historic lows due to the economic crisis. In the longer term, a Scotland growing faster than the UK and with a government in strict control of its finances will have a strong international credit rating. For all practical purposes, that will negate the problem of being tied to rUK base rates. Second issue: the Bank of England would not guarantee to buy Scottish Government bonds, as it does for UK debt at the moment. The No campaign argues that will make Scottish public borrowing relatively dearer, as there would be a higher theoretical risk. But the actual risk premium that a Scottish administration will pay for borrowing is directly linked to how responsible it is financially. This risk premium is usually measured by how much a government has to pay to borrow over what Germany has to pay

(Germany being the soundest risk). Measured on a typical day at the end of 2013, the UK Government paid +1.05 per cent over the German rate. But a host of well-managed, smaller European states paid far less: Austria (+0.35), Denmark (+0.08), Finland (+0.19), Netherlands (+0.32), and Sweden (+0.56). Even Ireland, with all its recent problems, had a risk premium of only +1.80, which is hardly extortionate. And Switzerland, whose banks in 2008 were in every bit as trouble as Britain's, now actually pays less for public borrowing than Germany! An independent Scotland that has sensibly reformed the chaotic UK tax system, is borrowing in a sustainable fashion, and which is growing faster than the rUK, will face a modest risk premium for state borrowing on a par with the other small European industrial nations.

But why, in the last resort, should the rUK want its second biggest trading partner to adopt a different currency? This would add around £500 million per annum to the business costs in rUK by making companies pay for currency conversions. Retaining a common sterling area also minimises the rUK's growing trade deficit. Taking Scotland out of sterling would add around £50 billion to rUK's trade gap. It would not be long before the markets punished any rUK government for running such a large and unsustainable trade imbalance. Ostensibly, George Osborne's main reservations about currency union concerns the (alleged) unequal contribution rUK would have to make to insure against bank failure. But after Scottish independence, the same big banks are likely to operate on both sides of the border – which implies that financial contagion is still possible regardless of the currency regime. This concrete fact suggests that – in the event of a Yes vote and Scotland's determination to continue using sterling – the monetary authorities in rUK will accept the necessity of negotiating common bank supervision and protection rules which form the basis of a sterling zone. The former Governor of the Bank of England, Mervyn King, had extensive and positive talks in this regard with Alex Salmond, which underlies the SNP's view that the Treasury will eventually agree to a common sterling zone. In January 2014, King's successor Mark Carney gave a speech in Edinburgh that fairly laid out the advantages and operational requirements of a currency union. He finished by saying the final decision was up to the governments of Scotland and rUK, and that the Bank (which would oversee any common currency zone) would act accordingly. Little noticed by the London media, Carney's speech began with a word of praise for his university academic supervisor and friend, James Mirrlees, the Nobel Prize-winning Scottish economist. Mirrlees is a key member of the Scottish Government's Fiscal Commission, which has produced a detailed blueprint for the operation of a common sterling zone. It was obvious from Carney's speech that he was acquainted with the work of the Fiscal Commission.[1]

## 2. Could Independent Scotland Pay Its Way?

Scotland is a rich country and there is no reason to imagine – in normal circumstances – that it could not fund its national budget at European levels of social provision. But Scotland is likely to become independent in circumstances that are anything but normal. Scotland will inherit a significant national debt from the UK Exchequer. Could it cope, especially if (as a new nation) it had to pay a substantial interest rate premium on its sovereign bonds?

Let us begin by stating that fiscal independence from Westminster is not about wanting to run a structural deficit – that's what Westminster does habitually. Scottish fiscal independence is about building a strong economy and that starts with creating a sustainable budget posture. Only that will create market confidence and sustain private investment at higher levels. Fiscal sustainability implies low risk on debt, as we noted above. It is true that the markets might – initially – attach a higher risk premium to any new state and government, especially one that has never before issued sovereign bonds. The SNP is wary of admitting this truism because the No campaign will immediately say it proves independence will raise interest rates permanently. Nothing of the sort follows. First, the international rating agencies have already downgraded the UK so staying in the Union hardly guarantees escape from a higher market risk premium. Second, the markets and ratings agencies will place a premium on past experience and this is very positive. Over the cumulative period 1980–81 to 2011–12, Scotland ran an average annual net fiscal surplus equivalent to 0.2 per cent of GDP. The UK, on the other hand, ran an average annual net fiscal deficit of 3.2 per cent of GDP. Third, at independence Scotland's budget situation would be far better than for the UK. In 2011–12 (the most recent year for which data is available) the UK had a deficit equivalent to 7.9 per cent of GDP. In comparison, Scotland ran a net fiscal deficit of 5.0 per cent. That is still above the EU's 3 per cent rule but on current trends the Scottish deficit will be below 3 per cent on independence – hardly grounds for the markets to attach a significant risk premium to Scottish bonds during any transitional period.

There is the question of Scotland's total stock of public debt on independence, and how the markets and ratings agencies will react to this in establishing the risk premium. UK public sector net debt at the end of 2011–12 stood at £1.1 trillion. Scotland's per capita share would have been equivalent to £92 billion (62 per cent of GDP). This would represent a lower debt to GDP ratio than for the UK as a whole (72 per cent), reflecting the fact that Scotland has a higher level of GDP per capita (including North Sea oil) than the UK. This is not to diminish the debt problem. But it is a debt problem bequeathed by the failed British state – another reason to vote Yes.

In November 2012, a report by the Institute of Fiscal Studies threw interesting light on the tax revenues contributed by the Scottish economy under the Union.[2] What jumps out is that the Scottish economy is being taxed at a higher proportion of income than the UK average. Ignoring North Sea taxes, 'onshore' tax revenues in 2010–11 were £45.2 billion, or 37.9 per cent of Scottish non-oil GDP. This compares with £542.9 billion, or 37.5 per cent of UK non-oil GDP. The immediate economic significance is that 'onshore' Scotland is bearing an above average share of the UK tax burden. (The gap is greater if we compare to UK GDP with oil.) However, as the IFS study also pointed out, 30 years ago Scotland's onshore revenues as a share of onshore GDP were even greater – a whole 3.3 percentage points higher

than those in the UK. What this means is that only a generation ago the relative weight and productivity of Scottish (non
oil) industry within the total UK economy was big enough
to yield a significantly higher tax income to the UK Treasury
than most other regions. That differential has been eroded
by relative economic decline in Scotland. Indeed, this higher
tax burden is yet another reason why Scottish growth under-
performed the UK average.

Had relative Scottish economic growth been maintained,
through a more fortuitous industrial mix, the proportion of
(non oil) tax receipts to GDP would be much higher than it
now is. If the tax receipts to GDP differential for Scotland
was still where it was 30 years ago – i.e. worth the equivalent of an extra 3 percentage points of GDP – the Scottish
economy would be generating about £4 billion more in
extra tax revenues. That would close the emerging fiscal
gap resulting from an ageing population, identified by the
IFS. A Yes vote is about creating the right circumstances to
re-industrialise the Scottish economy and recover the (non-
oil) level of public revenues generated in Scotland before
the London financial bubble.

## 3. What Happens when the Oil Runs Out?

Normally Scotland's substantial Atlantic and North Sea energy
resources would be taken as evidence that the independent
nation would prosper. But in the wake of the 2008 financial
crisis, opponents of a Yes vote have stood this argument on
its head. They argue that the volatility of tax revenues from oil

and gas would undermine budget stability. They also warn that high public spending and the need to reduce debt means oil revenues will be insufficient to create a Scottish equivalent of Norway's sovereign wealth fund – long a cherished SNP goal.

The revenue volatility argument is easily countered. True, the market price of oil can vary dramatically. But this is only a problem if – like the UK Treasury – a government plans to spend all its oil revenues without insuring against such swings. The solution – already advocated by the SNP Government – is to base budget projections on a rolling average of previous oil and gas revenues, and bank any excess that appears. The cumulative excess can then be used to create a buffer fund to be accessed if revenues in a particular year fall short. In this model, budget volatility would not depend on the peak and trough of oil prices themselves, but the deviation from the average tax income. Between the years 2000 and 2005, Scottish oil revenues averaged £3.9 billion per annum, with the worst year (2003–04) dropping to £3.4 billion, a variation of £488 million, or 1.1 per cent of that year's Scottish budget. That hardly counts as volatility. For the half decade to 2010, oil yielded an average annual income to Scotland of £6.4 billion – if we leave out 2008 when commodity prices rocketed before the Credit Crunch. The volatile year in this period was 2009–10, when the variation was £12.2 billion below average, or 2 per cent of the total Scottish budget. That's not negligible, but neither is it destabilising. And it was more than offset by the near doubling of oil revenues the year before.

The other contention is that, regardless of price, annual North Sea oil production and revenues are set to diminish in the near future. Accurate predictions in the oil business are rare and this area of debate is a political minefield. However, we will quote the acknowledged academic expert in the North Sea oil and gas industry, Professor Arnold Kemp of Aberdeen University, who is as politically neutral as it is possible to be in these matters:

> It can safely be concluded that substantial revenues from the upstream oil and gas sector would become available to a Scottish government, with a strong probability that they would fluctuate over the years. In the long run they will also decrease as production falls, but, as the results of our modelling above show there could be substantial production for many years ahead.[3]

It is true that production in UK waters fell by 40 percent between 2010 and 2013. But this was not due to North Sea oil running out. In a report published for the UK's own Energy Department in November 2013, industry veteran Sir Ian Wood estimated that 24 billion barrels of oil could still be produced, worth £1.6 trillion at current prices. Wood argued that output was being hindered because major oil companies were unwilling to lease equipment to smaller competitors in the North Sea, and because of high taxes. He made a series of proposals to deliver 3 or 4 billion more barrels of oil than would otherwise be recovered over the next 20 years. One point is obvious: an independent Scotland is more likely to create a tax and incentive regime to expand production, including public involvement Norwegian-style, than is any London administration.

However, the oil question is a red herring. Independent small economies in Europe are richer and have grown faster than Scotland in the past 30 years – despite having no oil resources, or indeed any great mineral bounty; e.g. Switzerland, Austria, Sweden and Finland. The gains from independence come not from oil but rather from the ability to raise productivity, investment and innovation to European levels once economic autonomy has been attained. North Sea oil revenues are a boon in this regard – if used wisely – in that they will shorten the transition period.

## 4. What Happens if the Banks Crash Again?

In a report published in 2013, the UK Treasury argues that 'the exceptionally large and highly-concentrated financial sector of an independent Scotland would be likely to increase the risks, to markets, firms and consumers, of financial services firms operating in an independent Scotland'.[4]

As an economic argument, this is frankly tendentious and mendacious. The argument that size should confer greater risk is not found in any economic textbook. Nor has a large, concentrated banking sector been bad for, say, Switzerland or Luxembourg. The Treasury paper argues that in an independent Scotland, the assets of domestic banks would equal 1,250 per cent of GDP. That random statistic is there to frighten the unwary, especially if compared to bankrupt Cyprus where the comparable figure is around 700 per cent. Of course, safe, dependable Luxembourg has bank assets worth 2,500 per cent of GDP, or double the Scottish figure.

In fact, Luxemburg has enjoyed social and economic stability since 1945 even though its banking sector provides one third of GDP and of tax revenues. Indeed, Luxemburg has the largest household wealth of any Western nation.

Sensing the Luxembourg case undermines their argument, the Treasury spin doctors clutch at straws. They claim Scotland 'would require to run large ... current account surpluses' in order to emulate Luxembourg's economic strength, to underwrite confidence in a large banking sector. But an independent Scotland would run a very large current account (trade) surplus. Oil and whisky would generate around £50 billion in exports annually. The rest of the UK – having lost Scottish export earnings – would see domestic interest rates rise in order to borrow the foreign currency needed to finance its massive trade deficit.

The point is that the size and concentration of a financial system is not a problem *per se* – the real issue is how well regulated it is. And the effectiveness of the regulatory regime has nothing to do with size and everything to do with the public authorities. Glaring example: it was the UK Treasury, as part of the triumvirate of British regulators, that failed miserably to head off the 2008 banking crisis. The self-same Treasury is now attempting to lecture an independent Scotland on financial prudence. It is true that had Scotland stuck to its traditional banking model, which eschewed banks borrowing on the wholesale money markets to find their own investment gambles, we would not have had the Credit Crunch. Indeed, the Canadian banks – still operating on those traditional Scottish banking principles – came unscathed through the global financial meltdown of 2008. The best reply to the

Treasury is that an independent Scotland will ban commercial banks from proprietary trading.

The Treasury paper also argues: 'There could be questions about an independent Scotland's ability to stabilise its banking system in the event of a future financial crisis.' As proof, it cites aid to RBS, noting that bank 'received £275 billion of guarantees through the UK Government's Asset Protection Scheme. This combined support from the UK Government to RBS is equivalent to some 211 per cent of Scottish GDP'. Readers are meant to draw the conclusion that wee Scotland can't protect its domestic depositors. The truth is that the Asset Protection Scheme did not involve any cash at all, far less multiples of Scottish GDP. It was an insurance scheme forced on RBS for which the bank paid the Treasury (i.e. which RBS depositors paid). In fact, RBS never called on a cent of the insurance payout because it was too expensive. If it had, the Treasury would merely have borrowed the cash on the financial markets and lent it on to RBS at a higher interest rate, thus making a profit.

There is one point repeated throughout the Treasury paper that is correct: that there is a 'tight relationship between the sovereign and bank's credit risk'. In lay terms, if a government is imprudent in borrowing, the markets will worry about the implications for the domestic banking sector. And the bigger a country's banking sector, the bigger the likely negative impact. The Treasury ghost writers interpret this as meaning Scottish banks will move their HQs to London to enjoy lower risk ratings and lower borrowing costs. Note the Treasury sleight-of-hand: the paper implies that an independent Scottish government would be imprudent in its borrowing. But as we noted earlier, over the period 1980–2012, an independent Scotland (with oil) would have run an annual average budget surplus. As for banks moving their HQs, the real threat comes from the likelihood that an alliance of the Tory right wing, the London tabloids and a populist UKIP will take the UK out of the European Union.

What would happen if a bank failed in Scotland? The Scottish Government would be liable for protecting depositors here, even if it was a subsidiary of an English bank. If a bank failed in England, the rUK Treasury would be responsible for insuring their deposits, even if it was a subsidiary of a Scottish-owned bank. This is because under European law every bank must be registered to operate in a given country (i.e. take local deposits). That country's authorities are then responsible for insuring their own depositors, even if it is a foreign bank. Had RBS failed under an independent Scotland, the English Treasury would have been legally bound to aid local English depositors. That said, after Scottish independence, in the event of a bank failing which had major operations on both sides of the Scottish-rUK border, one would expect a joint rescue operation by both governments, in the interests of maintaining confidence in the financial system.

<hr>

*Notes*

1   The members of the Fiscal Commission are Professors Andrew Hughes Hallett, Sir Jim Mirrlees, Frances Ruane and Joseph Stiglitz. It is chaired by Crawford Beveridge, former head of

RBS. The Commission's papers can be found on the Scottish Government website.

2 'Scottish independence: the fiscal context' by Paul Johnson and David Phillips, Institute for Fiscal Studies, November 2012.

3 Evidence to House of Commons Energy and Climate Change Committee, May 2012.

4 'Scotland analysis: Financial services and banking', UK Treasury, May 2013.

# THE MORAL ARGUMENT

## *Scotland Needs to Grow Up*

Most of the referendum debate is conducted in purely economic terms. In reality the case for independence is rooted in a profound moral argument. The legacy of the Union is a Scotland weakened by economic and political dependency. Independence aims to end that dependency culture by making Scotland and individual Scots stand on their own two feet. People living in a dependency culture are not free in mind, spirit or life choice even if they enjoy formal political liberties. Individuals in such a society have decisions taken for them *de facto* by the state or privileged interest groups. This is how the Labour Party apparatus ran much of urban Scotland from the 1930s onwards. No matter how well meant, the state paternalism bred by the Union during the twentieth century robbed Scotland of initiative and condemned those it pretended to help to poverty, ill health and social exclusion. It is high time Scots recovered their traditional veneration for hard work, thrift and personal responsibility – an outlook rooted deep in

Scottish history. That is best achieved by Scots creating their own state and paying their way out of their own taxes.

The heart of the moral case for voting Yes is based squarely on the idea of liberty – its beneficial effects on the individual and its retraining impact on the abuse of state power. However, this argument is not synonymous with modern economic neo-liberalism, or unrestrained individualism. Rather, it is an argument for independence based on the need to recover and put into practice traditional Scottish views on morality inherited from the Reformation and codified by Scottish Enlightenment thinkers such as Adam Smith and David Hume. This is a moral philosophy that definitely encourages private endeavour rather than state paternalism. But it also anchors private morality in a social context, in which the individual is empathetic to the outcome of his or her own conduct (or the conduct of others) on society as a whole. In other words, private virtue is evaluated by its impact on the greater good. The moral precepts of Scottish Enlightenment philosophy harnessed individual capitalist self-interest to nation-building and successful economic development, in the eighteenth and nineteenth centuries. In the latter years of the Union – hemmed in by a dependency culture on one side and individualistic greed on the other – Scotland lost sight of that moral compass. Witness the hubris that led to the collapse of RBS and HBOS in 2008, thereby grievously wounding a global reputation for banking probity in Scotland built up over 300 years. This is not a claim for Scottish moral superiority. It is an argument that says individual national communities have a unique historical experience that colours their view of the world and their place in it. Each national culture develops its own moral compass. Independence must involve nothing less than the recovery of Scotland's traditional moral universe, or it will fail.

There is a second, related moral argument for independence: Much of the No case is based implicitly on the notion that Scots are endemically poor or can't look after themselves and so need to be subsidised in perpetuity by the English taxpayer. Here is Treasury Secretary Danny Alexander, in November 2013, announcing that public spending per head in Scotland is higher than the UK average:

> These figures demonstrate that the people of Scotland continue to see a real financial benefit of over £1,300 per person compared to the UK average ... The UK remains the most successful economic and political union in history, and Scotland is one of its greatest success stories. It makes no sense to put this at risk through separation.

Either Mr Alexander, a Lib Dem, was trying to bribe Scots to stay in the Union, or he was implying they are too poor to stand on their own feet and needed English subsidy. The notion that Scottish society should seek, either deliberately or passively, to live at the expense of others is morally reprehensible and – in the long run – politically unsustainable. In essence, the No campaign is telling Scots voters to stick with the Union as a perpetual fiscal security blanket. Providing this supposed security blanket is what supports the material existence of Labour and the Liberal Democratic parties in Scotland because it funds their political 'clientelism'. Unionists will deny such as characterisation.

But ask yourself: when did a Conservative, Labour or Lib Dem politician ever outline a timetable to modernise the Scottish economy so that it no longer required financial subsidy from Westminster?

Unfortunately, the outcome of this clientelism poisons Scotland's reputation with the ordinary people of its southern neighbour and gives room for English demagogues to make ridiculous judgements about Scottish society. Listen to this (highly inaccurate) rant from Simon Heffer in the *Daily Mail* of 19 September 2013, which was not published in that newspaper's Scottish edition:

> Many Scots don't much like the English and appear ungrateful for everything that England does for them in showering them with money ... English money is propping up the most welfare, drink and drug-addicted nation in Europe ... Nowhere is public spending per head higher in the UK than in Scotland – where new road schemes, libraries, schools, hospitals and other state-of-the-art publicly-funded institutions are in an abundance rarely spotted in England.

In point of fact, official data disproves the notion that Scotland is subsidised financially by Westminster. According to the official Government Expenditure and Revenues Scotland (GERS) report, every year for the 30 years to 2010–11, Scotland has generated more tax revenue per head for the UK Treasury than the UK average, assuming Scotland's share of North Sea oil revenues. GERS data also shows that in 2010–11, Scotland generated 9.9 per cent of the UK tax revenue but received only 9.3 per cent of public spending. It is true that (identifiable) public spending per head is higher in Scotland than the UK average, by some £1,300 per annum in 2012–13. But this reflects higher unit costs in Scotland associated with meeting UK levels of service provision; e.g. a low population density compared with the English South; maintaining roads in an area one third of the UK landmass; and tackling Scotland's unique health issues. However, the London region also consistently has a higher than average public spend per capita. This does not reflect gains by the local citizens. Rather, public spending in London reflects the need to support its vast transport infrastructure and pretensions to be a global capital: spending on the culture and the arts in London is fifteen times greater per head than in the other English regions. London's per capital premium on spending *vis-à-vis* England is of the same order as that of Scotland relative to the UK figure, but for less defensible reasons.

Yet even supposing Scotland was being subsidised by England that would not be an argument for voting No. If it were proved that Scotland had a so-called structural fiscal deficit – that it was forever dependent on London handouts – that would be a most persuasive argument for independence. First, because England does not deserve to be exploited in perpetuity. And second, because forever depending on handouts destroys self-respect.

## Recovering Scotland's Traditional Moral Universe

The importance of public morality in Scottish society explains why Scotland's middle classes rejected Thatcherism and began to turn to supporting independence. At first sight Margaret Thatcher would seem to embody the values of thrift, hard work and individual responsibility that characterise the traditional world view of those same Scottish middle classes. But the Scottish historical psyche (built on Presbyterian guilt) has also been taught to repudiate – at least in public – greed, hedonism, ostentation, and the sort of individualism that denies duty to something higher. In the Scots Calvinist universe, wealth creation and using one's individual talents have nothing to do with maximising personal gain. Rather they are how one does one's duty to God (however defined). By seeming to ignoring this crucial moral precept in favour of a more hedonistic individualism, Mrs Thatcher failed to win over Middle Scotland. Of course, there is room for lots of hypocrisy and cynicism in this Scottish approach to politics. Individual Scots are not morally superior to anyone else nor are their elected politicians. But a unique history has bequeathed Scots a particular cultural norm for making collective political judgements – a measuring stick that is different from England. On the basis of that peculiarly Scottish approach, the current Union finds itself wanting.

Today, most Scots share the secular outlook of their fellow Britons. However, a distinct moral outlook remains embedded in the nation's cultural DNA. This is because, for some 250 years, Scotland's separate university system has routinely transmitted the moral philosophy of the Scottish Enlightenment to its students, and the latter have gone on to serve as the middle-class cadres staffing Scottish politics, business, medicine, education and the Church. In a sense, this Enlightenment moral philosophy codifies in secular terms the earlier Calvinist notions of worshipping the Creator through hard work and service to others in ordinary daily life. Central to this codification is Adam Smith's *Theory of Moral Sentiments*, published in 1759. The great Scottish philosopher is more famous outside of Scotland for his book *The Wealth of Nations*, which first synthesised the workings of a free-market economy. Smith's economic inquiries were only part of a wider scientific analysis of how human society functioned and how it functioned best. He argued that public morality – meaning the set of rules that allow complex human societies to function well – is not secured by 'the multiplication of laws', or by the intervention of government. He believed (with good cause) that both the legal system and politicians are eminently corruptible. Rather, Smith argued that public morality is secured at the private level, in each individual via the cultivation of his or her own moral sensibilities. These sensibilities include 'sympathy, empathy and solidarity' with the rest of the community. Native individualism is tempered by worrying about what society thinks – a very Scottish trait.

Right-wing Unionists and some libertarians have long been perplexed by the rejection of Thatcherism by Scotland's middle class. Equally, middle-class Scots – educated in Scottish moral philosophy at Scottish universities – never saw Mrs Thatcher as one of their own. The Scottish middle class are not socialists – they read Adam Smith's *Wealth of Nations* at university as well. But the Scottish moral universe – a reflection of its post-Reformation Presbyterian culture and Enlightenment philosophy – revolves around the ethos of service to some greater good. This is where Thatcherite individualism failed to chime with Scottish middle-class sensibilities. Thatcher was good at pulling down but hopeless at building up. She destroyed not just the trade unions but a whole industrial ecology – skills, communities, relationships – on which Scottish manufacturing was based. What she put in its place was not a new manufacturing economy able to pay its own way in the world and fund a decent welfare system. Instead she bequeathed Britain a phoney consumer culture based on unsustainable levels of debt. In the 1979 referendum on Scottish devolution, only 40 per cent of middle-class voters supported the 'assembly' as it was then called. Post Thatcher, in 1997, 69 per cent of the middle-class voted Yes to a Scottish Parliament. It was this defection of the Scots middle class that changed the political balance – working-class electors voted in favour on both occasions by 57 and 91 per cent respectively. After Thatcher, Blair and Brown had the historic opportunity to change direction. Instead, they took the Thatcherite economic model to its logical conclusion. It is this suspect moral universe that Scotland seeks to escape through independence.

The recovery of a traditional national moral compass would have a profound impact on Scotland's politics after independence. In a speech in China, in December 2011, Alex Salmond came his closest to defining the SNP's foreign policy. Explicitly citing Smith's *Theory of Moral Sentiments* (reputedly a favourite of China's then Premier, Wen Jiabao), Salmond said his political watchwords were 'sympathy, empathy and solidarity', claiming a 'moral' approach to international relationships – moral not in the sense of 'good' but of understanding that being part of a global free trade economy brings responsibilities as well as rights. Salmond went on to argue that lasting trade partnerships can only be achieved if rich Scotland appreciates the problems, needs and aspirations of other nation states – Smith's 'sympathy, empathy and solidarity'. For example, Scotland pioneered the carbon-fuelled industrial economy, so it has a moral duty to help fix climate change. Only then can Scotland expect to sell renewables to Beijing. In a neat phrase, Salmond called this approach 'sharing ambitions'. This is a very different approach from David Cameron who combined public attacks on China's human rights record (of questionable moral import given the UK's colonial record in that country in the nineteenth century) with arrogant demands that Beijing 'buy British'. Salmond's 'sympathetic approach' (putting yourself in the other's shoes) is a very different starting point from the traditional naked self-interest model promulgated by the British Foreign Office, and therefore likely to be more successful in the long run.

## Objection 1: Independence Would Mean Big Government and Tax-and-Spend Politics

This is the 'moral' objection to independence from the Unionist right wing: Scottish independence is more likely to entrench state interference and loss of liberty than to promote it.

It would be wrong to ignore the fact that decades of social dependency under Scottish Labour has made a section of the Scottish people dependent on the state, or that the destruction of Scottish manufacturing under the Union since 1945 has left a worryingly large percentage of GDP in the hands of the state. But the solution is to free Scotland from Westminster's apron strings and make it responsible for its own finances. The natural libertarian and free-market stance should be to favour small nations with reduced bureaucracy and more transparent and accountable government.

Rightly, most people now reject the authoritarian paternalist state of the extreme Left and Right, with its bureaucracy and lack of human rights. But the liberal democratic state has its own peculiar defects. To understand this we might look to the work of the contemporary Irish political philosopher Philip Pettit. He makes the distinction between a state based on guaranteeing non-domination of the individual and one based on protecting individuals from interference with making choices, especially economic ones. The latter version of 'liberty' is now all-pervasive. But as Pettit points out, it is easily corrupted into sanctioning the worst excess of the free-market economy while rendering the majority powerless and dependent. Hence the collapse in social mobility in the UK. Hence the virtual economic dictatorship by City bankers. Hence, even, the buying of cherished football clubs by foreign oligarchs.

Any future Scottish state should be based on the principle of non-domination. This has more in common with traditional Scottish moral and political philosophy than contemporary neo-liberalism. In such a 'republic of equals', the institutions of the state would guarantee the individual more than just the freedom to make their own private choices, as in the Thatcherite version of neo-liberalism. Here the state would also ensure that each citizen is emancipated from the threat of undue dependence, be it economic, cultural, or political. Such a state worries about the dispiritedness that affects men and women who lead dependent lives as much as it worries about the rate of GDP growth. This has concrete implications: it requires radical public intervention to protect citizens from monopoly or discrimination. This should not be interpreted as a call for intervention in the market place, but it is a declaration of war on inherited privilege and vested interests. The non-domination principle leads immediately to the conclusion that Scotland cannot control its economic destiny or fulfil the potential of its people if it remains tied to the dictates of a failed banking system run by (and for) the City of London. This new state envisages no levelling down, no Stalinist social engineering. It will favour the traditional Scottish lad (and lassie) o' pairts – ambitious, educated, entrepreneurial. But unlike the Thatcherite, neo-liberal model, the principle of non-domination imposes on the state the task of nurturing individual talent in the first place.

Such a state demands a very active public role from its citizens. Is this vision of the future Scottish state too abstract for the contemporary electorate brought up in a consumer culture? If so, democracy itself is doomed except as a fig leaf for the rich. Besides, you don't vote nations into being by appealing to the lowest common denominator.

## Objection 2: Cutting Taxes in an Independent Scotland Initiates a Race to the Bottom

The 'moral' objection from the left toward independence is that an SNP government will be characterised by crude, neo-Thatcherite policies, particularly making deep cuts in corporation tax to attract foreign investment, and that this will force rUK to follow suit. The result will be 'a race to the bottom' as everyone cuts tax rates, yielding no economic benefits and reducing public revenues. Gordon Brown denounced SNP plans for lower corporation tax, arguing: 'nationally varied corporation tax rates … will start a race to the bottom under which the good provider in one area would be undercut by the bad and the bad would be undercut by the worst.'

It is true the SNP will use tax-varying powers to attract foreign capital and stimulate domestic investment. Yet academic studies have found scant evidence that such policies result in a competitive 'race to the bottom'. On the contrary, empirical evidence points in the direction that tax competition actually helps economic growth all round. By way of proof, national tax revenues from corporate profits have remained fairly stable across the industrial world, relative both to GDP and total tax revenue. If there had been a race to the bottom, we'd have seen such revenues decline. The explanation is simple: economies have their own peculiarities, so perforce they require different tax requirements. Left to themselves, they will establish a tax regime that fits their needs – helping each to compete effectively. They will not just cut taxes willy-nilly. On the other hand, enforced tax harmonisation between nations and regions inevitably means a sub-optimal fiscal policy. And because tax harmonisation is usually imposed by the stronger party the smaller economy inevitably is disadvantaged. Think about the Treasury's desperate attempts to stop the devolution of corporation tax to Northern Ireland and you'll get the point. These findings have led Paul Krugman, the Nobel Prize-wining economist, to propose a tax floor to stop big countries forcing smaller countries to set corporate tax rates higher than is good for their economies, as Germany and France want to do to Ireland.

## Conclusion

Morals count. The one key area where a return to Scottish moral precepts is long overdue is in banking. In the eighteenth century, Scots invented the overdraft and pioneered a model of responsible retail banking that encouraged savings and entrepreneurship. They exported this model to other countries, including Canada. Scottish investors still took risks but in real things with a real return. During the 2008 financial crisis, Canadian banks were largely unaffected because they stuck to the Scots model of retail lending rather than gamble on the derivatives markets with borrowed money. In Scotland RBS and HBOS had broken with their roots – with disastrous results. Unionists argue against independence because Scotland could not have dealt with the banking failures on its own. On the contrary, the implosion of RBS and HBOS was the result of Scotland losing its moral anchor. The solution is to find it again by voting Yes.

# 5

# THE INTERNATIONALIST ARGUMENT

## An Independent Scotland Adds to the World

In a famous phrase, the SNP's first Member of the European Parliament, Winnie Ewing, said: 'Stop the world – Scotland wants to get on'. Sovereignty would give Scotland increased diplomatic and economic manoeuvrability, which is a precious asset in an increasingly globalised world. It would also be good for the world.

An independent Scotland would rank 117th by population among states and autonomous territories. Even inside the EU, 19 of the current 27 member states have a population that is greater than Scotland's. Size is also related to land area. An independent Scotland would come 118th among nations by area, though ahead of the Netherlands, Belgium and Denmark. However, economic muscle counts most in the size stakes. Here an independent Scotland rises in the league tables. Measuring GDP per capita, including a geographical share of North Sea oil and gas revenues, Scotland easily ranks among the top 20 economies, though somewhere in the bottom half. Scotland is neither a microstate nor a super power. But it belongs squarely to the family of rich, educated, technological societies found in the OECD and EU. As such, an independent Scotland would have some consequence in the world, on a par with the likes of Norway, Denmark or Sweden. The SNP is also committed to joining the EU and NATO, giving the new state leverage in the main Western alliances.

The counter-argument is that big nations such as the UK – with their large populations, superior capital endowment and economies of industrial scale – have more clout in the world than smaller ones, particularly in times of crisis. It is also claimed that the demand of Scotland, Catalonia, the Basque Country and the Flemish part of Belgium to form independent states inherently weakens the ability of the EU to act collectively in a crisis. From this perspective, Scottish society gains more from being part of the collective UK, where the constitution is flexible enough to let Scotland use the diplomatic weight of the British state to express its own interests on a European and global stage.

However, the truth is that larger nations do not necessarily dictate events. On the contrary, the recent financial meltdown and global recession actually originated inside the bigger US and UK economies. And the UK, while it had a big enough financial sector in the City of London to trigger the Credit Crunch, is actually a mid-sized power with relatively limited ability to dictate global diplomatic direction. The UK is generally a loyal follower of whatever policy is being pursued by the White House. In fact, there is an emerging view that small industrial economies such as Scotland possess a unique set of advantages when it comes to navigating the globalised economy, as compared to large nations. The United Nations Industrial Development Organisation maintains: 'Small highly dynamic economies are displacing mature, developed countries as global industrial competitors.'

Small economies of the European industrial kind tend to be more export-focused than larger ones. This follows from the smaller size of their domestic market relative to GDP. Small countries are not just 'structurally open', they are also 'functionally open' in the sense that they pursue trade openness as a conscious policy choice; e.g. the tax-cutting fiscal competition exhibited by Ireland and Sweden. Economic efficiency demands that small industrial economies concentrate on only a few product or service lines, so they specialise in niches that are too small for large nations to fill comfortably. This ability of small nations to exploit niche export markets has been increased by the emergence of global supply chains and the ease with which technology is transferred – meaning that small countries can build competitive advantage in making high value components. Call this the 'small state globalisation' model.

The two undoubted success stories of small state globalisation are the Netherlands and Switzerland. They have parlayed their export success into the creation of powerful global companies; e.g. Shell, Phillips, Heineken, and Unilever in Holland, and Nestle, Zurich, Credit Suisse, Roche, Novartis, UBS, and ABB in Switzerland. Thus lack of political clout is compensated for by commercial clout. It is a model that can be replicated; viz. the success of the Gorenje company in Slovenia, which now has a 5 per cent share of Europe's kitchen appliance market. Small industrial economies are also big foreign investors. Surprising as it may be, Denmark's overseas direct investment is on the same scale as China's. And the financial markets of Luxembourg and Switzerland control a larger proportion of US sovereign debt than does China. Beijing may have a huge sovereign wealth fund that it can use for diplomatic leverage, but the China Investment Corporation had assets at the start of 2013 of only $482 billion compared with $667 billion in Norway's equivalent.

The small state globalisation model means more than being efficient manufacturers or big foreign investors. It is also about education and innovation, the *sine qua non* of the contemporary global economy. Small industrial economies with a commitment to cultural pluralism and immigration can provide a sympathetic context for fostering divergent thinking and creativity. Small size favours debate and learning.

The final component of the small state globalisation model has to do with adaptability. Small nations are certainly vulnerable to exogenous shocks but they are therefore much better at adapting to change and implementing structural reform. Finland lost 15 per cent of its GDP in three years, after the collapse of the Soviet Union destroyed its main export market. But Finnish growth soon bounced back and by 2000 was a phenomenal 6 per cent as the Finns went into the mobile phone business. Iceland's banks failed in 2008, sending unemployment up to 10 per cent. But by 2012 Iceland had recovered and unemployment was below 5 per cent. Swedish economic growth hit a record low in 2008 but was back at an all-time high by 2010. In 2008, Switzerland had to bail out its banks, which had liabilities several times larger than the country's GDP. Within a few years the Swiss authorities were desperately trying to stop hot money flows from the stricken Eurozone pouring into their country's restored banking system. Overall, the majority of small nations in Western Europe made a faster and stronger recovery from the 2008 Credit Shock than did the UK. How?

These countries were able to tailor fiscal policy to their own local needs. A bigger nation may have superior borrowing powers but its fiscal policy ends up a compromise that may not suit specific regions (e.g. Scotland) when it comes to promoting recovery. Ireland's export-led recovery was predicated on its low corporation tax. Sweden returned to growth by slashing income tax, especially for low-income families. Iceland refused to bail out its banks with taxpayers' money and banned the export of capital to ensure bank funds were invested in the local economy.

There is a final interesting twist to the small nation globalisation idea: the so-called 'flotilla effect' of small nations working together to offset the power of larger nations. The increase in the number of new nations since the Second World War is a commonplace observation. But more nations mean the global power wielded by larger states is to a degree defused by competition from the new, particularly if these new nations are rich economically, technologically and culturally, as is Scotland. One extra polity like Scotland has a limited competitive impact. But the arrival of the Baltic States, Slovenia, Scotland, Catalonia, and the Basque Country does have a potential impact, especially on Europe. This may explain the enthusiasm of the Dutch entrepreneur

Freddie Heineken for 'Eurotopia', his vision of a network of 75 small, historic European nations and regions, as the economic future.

## Objection 1: Could an Independent Scotland Defend Itself?

The argument for remaining inside the UK stresses the extra security – against military, terrorist and criminal threats – afforded by being part of the larger British state.

Such threats cannot be dismissed. Scotland was at the receiving end of a foiled terrorist bomb attack at Glasgow Airport in 2007. And while a major physical threat to an independent Scotland seems unlikely, small nations are certainly subject to bullying by bigger ones, even in Europe. Witness the Russian incursion into Georgia in 2008, the mysterious cyber-attack on Latvia in 2007 that probably originated from a section of the Russian intelligence apparatus, and the friction between Russian and Ukraine over the latter's moves towards association with the European Union. In 2010 RAF Tornado aircraft from Leuchars in Fife were being scrambled on average twice a month to intercept Russian Tu-160 bombers and escort them away from Scottish airspace.

In addition, an independent Scotland would face specific geopolitical security issues as a result of its North Atlantic location. These include protecting the West of Shetland and North Sea oil fields, managing international competition over maritime resources and navigation rights, and providing Scotland's share of defence duties on NATO's northern flanks – an agenda which is probably more taxing than that faced by many other small nations. As the twenty-first-century progresses, the melting of the Greenland and Arctic ice caps will add to this complex picture. Climate change has the potential to open up the Northeast Passage to shipping between Europe and Asia, and allow the exploitation of minerals and fossil fuels previously trapped under the ice. Within a generation the focus of global maritime transport could switch to the seas just north of Scotland. The emergence of this new strategic theatre presents Scotland with opportunities and threats.

However, the supposed strategic security blanket Scotland enjoys as part of the United Kingdom is more theoretical than real. Recent Westminster governments have ignored Scottish defence requirements. There is practically no conventional naval warfare presence left in Scotland, which accounts for half of Britain's seacoast. The 2010 Coalition Government defence review closed the RAF fighter base at Leuchars and all of the UK's Nimrod maritime reconnaissance planes were scrapped leaving no air cover over the North Sea and Atlantic for the first time since the Second World War. Defence cuts mean Scotland will be reduced to one naval base (for Trident nuclear submarines), one military airfield (but no patrol planes to protect oil fields and fisheries), and less troops stationed locally than has the Slovenian army.

Despite this highly risky reduction in UK defence capability – overall and particularly in Scotland – the Conservative Secretary of State for Defence, Philip Hammond, had the temerity to come north of the border to lecture the SNP on the dangers of independence. With no evidence, he claimed that soldiers in an independent Scotland would not have 'access to the quality of kit and equipment with which they currently operate'. This from the head of a Ministry of Defence that sent British troops to fight and die in Iraq and Afghanistan without decent armoured personnel carriers, radios or infrared night-vision scopes, and without sufficient helicopters. Hammond also tried a weak joke by saying 'half a destroyer would be no use to anyone, neither would be one frigate' – inferring that Scotland's share of UK naval assets would be too small to provide a credible force. But the joke is on Mr Hammond and the miniscule conventional Royal Navy he commands. In 2014 Britain had no proper aircraft carriers and only five destroyers and thirteen frigates – hence the 'half' destroyer and 'one' frigate due to Scotland on a population basis.

The idea that Scotland, a rich nation with a martial tradition, could not – or would not – defend itself is risible. A more pertinent question is why the MoD has been so militarily cack-handed since the Second World War despite the bravery and sacrifice of ordinary soldiers, sailors and aviators? The answer lies in the delusions of imperial grandeur of Westminster politicians. Billions are still being wasted on a pointless nuclear deterrent decades after the Cold War ended – meaning there isn't the cash to kit the troops with proper conventional equipment. True, Scotland's naval force would be small to start with, but only because the UK's is already microscopic. The Norwegian navy, the best comparator for an independent Scotland, operates five frigates, six corvettes and six submarines – far greater coastal protection than Scotland gets from the Royal Navy at the moment. Scotland would actually be better defended if it relied on its own wits. At least we might get some maritime reconnaissance planes to protect our shipping lanes.

## Objection 2: Would Scotland Have to Renegotiate EU Membership?

In February 2013, Jose Manuel Barroso, President of the European Commission, claimed that it would be 'extremely difficult, if not impossible' for an independent Scotland to join the European Union. Is he right?

If Scotland can't be a member of the EU, it is difficult to see who else would meet the membership criteria. Scotland has impeccable European credentials, joining the then European Common Market along with the other nations of the UK back in 1973. Of the 28 current members of the EU, the vast majority (19) in fact joined after Scotland. With 41 years of membership, Scotland complies with all the many rules – legal, economic, political and social – required of each EU member state. Scots have long been at the centre of promoting European collaboration: David Maxwell Fyfe, a canny Scots lawyer, was instrumental in drafting the European Convention on Human Rights. Given this background, the SNP contends that following independence Scotland would be fast-tracked to separate membership status in the EU. Even if, for the sake of argument, Scotland did have to apply formally for EU membership under Article 49 of the Constitutional Treaty, it would still remain in *de facto* membership of the EU, as they wouldn't yet be 'independent'.

Certainly there need to be discussions over Scotland's financial contribution and voting rights but the same would go for the down-sized remainder of the UK. Such a tidying up operation could surely be done in parallel with the negotiations being conducted between Holywood and Westminster regarding independence itself.

Of course, political life is not so simple. There are vested interests that want to make the process of formalising EU membership and de-merging from the UK more difficult for Scotland than it need be, or should be. However the creation of such roadblocks – real or imaginary – has nothing whatsoever to do with Scotland's ability to be a good EU member, comply with EU rules, or play a constructive role in European affairs. Most of the screaming headlines warning that an independent Scotland would face the prospect of loss of EU membership are found in London newspapers that are themselves rabidly anti-European. Consistency might suggest these periodicals advocate a Yes vote if they think Scotland would really find itself out of the EU.

How seriously should we take the threat from Mr Barroso that an independent Scotland would find itself outside of the EU? Or what of the warning from Mariano Rajoy, the Spanish Prime Minister: 'I know for sure that a region that would separate from a member state of the European Union would remain outside the European Union and that should be known by the Scots and the rest of the European citizens.' Neither Mr Rajoy, nor Mr Barroso (a former Prime Minister of Portugal with close political friendships in Spain) are concerned with the facts of Scotland's European credentials. Scotland was an EU member while both Iberian states were still dictatorships. Barroso and Rajoy's threat to force an independent Scotland out of the EU has nothing to do with Scotland and everything to do with blackmailing Catalan democrats into dropping their threat to hold their own independence referendum. The old Francoist right in Spain still exists and is making grumbling noises about a coup if the uppity Catalans exercise their democratic right to vote on self-determination. A desperate Mr Rajoy is using Scotland as a stick to beat the Catalans, and Barroso is help-ing him. They would be better advised to use the example of Scottish democracy in action as a way of isolating the fascists. The legal reality is that there is nothing in the EU treaties that covers a member state dissolving into its constituent parts. Politicians such as Mr Rajoy and EU civil servants such as Mr Barroso can express personal opinions but the only con-stitutional body that can adjudicate on the treaties is the European Court of Justice. As it is, the likelihood of Spain actually exercising a veto on Scottish membership is virtually zero. The Catalan referendum is scheduled for 18 December 2014. By the time Scotland becomes formally independent (say 2016) the Catalan issue will have been resolved one way or another.

Those tempted to vote No in order to safeguard Scottish membership of the EU face another contradiction – the pros-pect of a UK-wide referendum on EU membership promised by David Cameron and the Conservatives if they return to office in 2015. According to opinion polls which use the exact wording in the Tory draft bill for such an EU referen-dum, only 36 per cent of UK electors will vote to stay in, trumped by 45 per cent who will vote to leave. That means even if Scots stick with the UK in September 2014, the likelihood is that English voters will take Britain out of the EU anyway. The anti-European London press will be whooping for joy – the very same press that keeps trying to frighten Scots voters with dark tales about how difficult it will be for Alex Salmond to negotiate continued EU membership.

Even if Scotland were outside the EU, life would not end. Indeed, polls indicate that many Scots have grown more wary of the EU since the start of the Eurozone crisis and German-imposed austerity. Gordon Wilson, a respected former SNP leader, and Jim Sillars, the party's former deputy leader, argue an independent Scotland should open negotiations to join the European Free Trade Area (Efta). There are four non-EU countries presently in Efta: Norway, Switzerland, Liechtenstein and Iceland. They share an 'internal market' with the EU, giving the advantages of free trade without the burdens of membership. Another alternative is joining the North American Free Trade Agreement (Nafta), which links Canada, the US and Mexico. Nafta operates more like an ordinary free trade zone than a blueprint for political union.

In America they worry that Scottish and Catalan independence will balkanise Europe and weaken the EU. The reverse is true. Until the mid-1990s the EU had a project for a 'Europe of the Regions' in which greater autonomy at the level of small nations would counter-balance power in Brussels. This sensible model was subverted by the big member states, leading to the present domination of Berlin and its suicidal (for Europe) fixation with austerity. Far from balkanising Europe, the independence movements in Scotland and Catalonia are the best route to overcoming the EU's democratic deficit.

# 6

# THE CULTURAL ARGUMENT

*Scotland Needs to Express Itself*

Since the fall of the Iron Curtain at the beginning of the 1990s – arguably the start of the latest wave of globalisation – some thirty-four new nation states have come into being. Clearly the contention that globalisation is making nations less important is wrong. On the contrary, in a trading world of 7 billion souls, possessing a distinctive national culture – open and experimental, yet providing a sense of place – is more necessary than ever to economic success. Perhaps even to survival. The most effective national cultures attract and mobilise talent from across the globe, yet provide a stable identity for individuals and groups. An independent Scotland – free to talk directly to the rest of the world in its own cultural terms – would be just such a place.

Put another way, twenty-first-century globalisation needs cultural diversity – in education, artistic experiment, freedom of debate, and sexual expression – the way the natural world requires biodiversity for survival and regeneration. The alternative is cultural assimilation by big nation states, the resulting political friction and eventual global cultural stasis. Globalisation and the Internet have created a giant market for cultural products and ideas. Paradoxically however, cultural production (scientific as well as artistic) still thrives on proximity and human interchange as much as mass markets and instant global communications. And cultural creativity is stimulated best through artistic communities and networks – the intimate communities provided best of all in cities and small nations. Far from being parochial – a frequent criticism of British Unionists towards Scottish independence – small, industrial nations have been havens for immigrant artists and cultural experimentation. Scotland is a prime example – independence would make it more so.

## Scotland – a Unique Culture

Even inside the strictures of the Union, Scottish culture has been remarkably open. A singular and recurrent internationalism has profoundly marked all levels of Scottish society. This is a set of emotional ties with the rest of the world different from those England enjoys, in terms of geography and in the sense of being strongly personal rather than institutional. England's external world view is conditioned by its long historical antipathy to Continental Europe. English cultural motifs centre on being an insular, embattled island (with a country park at its spiritual centre) – curious, because England isn't an island. Scotland's world view is conditioned by its traditional economic role – from early medieval times till the nineteenth century – as Europe's crossroads between the Baltic north and the Mediterranean south; by its experience as a French dependency before 1560; and by the forced mass emigration of its sons and daughters in the twentieth century. As a result, Scotland is perhaps the most culturally diverse nation in northern Europe, and has been for a century or more.

Fully one-third of contemporary Scots are of recent Irish decent. Italian immigrants from Picinisco and Barga in the early twentieth century revolutionised Scottish eating habits and its cultural tastes: nobody in Scotland thinks of Richard Demarco or Eduardo Paolozzi as anything but Scottish artists. (Both Edinburgh born, Demarco helped found the famous avant-garde Traverse Theatre in the early 1960s, while Paolozzi became famous for his sculpture.) East European Jews fleeing the pogroms arrived in Scotland before the First World War. Many thought they had paid passage for New York only to find unscrupulous ship owners had disembarked them at Leith and not Ellis Island. Fortunately they stayed and added richly to twentieth-century Scottish life: the family of Malcolm Rifkind, Secretary of State for Scotland under Margaret Thatcher, arrived from Lithuania in the 1890s. The Second World War brought over 100,000 Poles and Ukrainians escaping Stalin's rape of their countries – an equivalent immigration into England would scale up to a million or more. Another 100,000 Poles came at the start of the twenty-first century. The Sixties and Seventies brought new Scots from the Asian sub-continent, from Uganda and from Hong Kong. And in 1973 came the refugees from Pinochet's Chile. This Scottish melting pot is one of the reasons that the concept of Britain no longer works. Scots have already forged a new, non-British sense of identity as a way of integrating these diverse peoples. This explains why modern Scottish Nationalism so obviously has nothing to do with tartanry and Balkan-style revanchism. It was perforce a civic affair on a par with the creation of Canadian or Australian identities distilled out of immigrant communities.

None of this came easily. We should not be blind to our own human frailties. The long Protestant-Catholic divide, an anti-Irish vendetta based on jobs insecurity, scarred the nation for generations. The gentle Italian community suffered its own Kristallnacht on Leith Walk in 1940 when Mussolini declared war. Asian citizens have met with racial prejudice no less than elsewhere. But overall, the traditional Scottish vision of a moral community; the sanity of a small nation where most everybody is a recent arrival; the levelling effect of a heterogeneous social mix; the socialist internationalism of the trades unions, and the democratic intellect of a home-brewed intelligentsia rather than Oxbridge elitism; all these have combined to produce at the start of the twenty-first century a modern, civic identity, not a pseudo-ethnic one. This Scottish melting pot maintained direct links with the rest of the world via its own non-British channels. The Church of Scotland, the Catholic Church and a heavily Communist-influenced trade union movement all conducted their own foreign policy independent of Whitehall. The Church of Scotland virtually ran large parts of Africa. The Scottish universities still train the Commonwealth's doctors, using a wholly Scottish approach to medicine. Scots artists, from the pre-First War Colourists in France to the later New Glasgow

Expressionists in New York, showed a profound intellectual interest in everywhere except London.

The genesis of modern Scottish nationalism grew out of this profoundly cosmopolitan spirit, long held in check by the narrow confines of British imperial insularity. Contemporary Scottish nationalism in the shape of the SNP (founded in 1934) emerged as a part of the European Modernist movement born of the 1920s. Many of the writers, architects, documentary filmmakers, and artists involved in the development of Scottish Modernism were involved in the creation of the SNP. Chief among these was the poet, critic and socialist Christopher Grieve, who wrote under the pseudonym of Hugh MacDiarmid. The Scottish Modernists by-passed London to create links with Modernists in Continental Europe, especially in the new wave of small nations that emerged after the First World War.

Why was Modernism – a self-conscious rejection of the hierarchical, bourgeois societies of the nineteenth century – more influential in Scotland than England? In part, the internationalism, abstraction and interconnectedness of Modernism appealed to intellectuals brought up in the more generalist and theoretical discourse of the ancient Scottish universities (as opposed to Oxbridge). In part, Modernism arrived at the right historical moment for those seeking a break with an older, conservative Scotland that had already appropriated Burns and tartanry for its cultural legitimacy. In part, Marxism as a competitor to Modernism had limited roots in Scotland. Above all, a political project of national regeneration – for once the term 'modernisation' is appropriate – had a unique resonance during a period of economic decline to which the Imperial Parliament in London had no obvious answer, either in the Great Depression or after 1945.

The period from the 1970s to the devolution referendum in 1997 saw a second great wave of creative energy in the arts in Scotland, especially in theatre and literature. With de-industrialisation and Westminster's rejection of the 1979 referendum majority, Scotland's cultural community became the centre of political resistance against Thatcherism, literally forging a modern, non-British identity for the nation. It was not long before politics followed in the wake of this cultural revolution. On the wall of the new Scottish Parliament building at the bottom of Edinburgh's Royal Mile is a quote from novelist Alasdair Gray which sums up the mood engendered by this cultural upheaval: 'Work as if you live in the early days of a better nation'.

Unlike in England, Scottish politics have been uniquely influenced by writers, poets and artists. More importantly, these creatives had an open, internationalist outlook – not an introverted, pseudo-ethnic one. The nation's artists, because of their education in the humanist tradition of the Scottish Enlightenment, retain the view that social progress is not only possible but desirable. It is this positive outlook which would find an even greater freedom expression in an independent Scotland. The result would be a better, more interesting place to live and a nation that would contribute manifold benefits to the global community.

## Objection 1: Independent Scotland Would be Culturally Dominated by America and England

The dominant view of national sovereignty implies that big nations (e.g. the USA) can exert cultural hegemony through their larger resources and control over new technology. Thus Hollywood, Facebook and Google set the cultural global agenda which small nations are powerless to influence, except on the margins. For an independent Scotland, which is part of the Anglophone world, there would be few barriers to US and English cultural penetration. In this view, independence is the shortcut either to cultural domination by external forces, or to a withering parochialism.

However, it is hard to defend the proposition that Ireland has been culturally assimilated. On the contrary, Ireland proves that being part of the Anglophone community can be a strategic asset that Scotland would share. And like Ireland, Scotland has access to a large diaspora as a means of reinforcing its global image and position following independence. Scotland is among the major migrant nations of modern times. Currently around 20 per cent of the Scottish-born population live outside the homeland while some estimates put Scotland's entire diaspora at 40 million (Scottish Government, 2009). Much of this diaspora is concentrated in North America, which is a rich source of business contacts, political influence and capital that would allow Scotland to exert more influence than is suggested by her modest domestic population.

In fact, globalisation is actually creating a new market for international cultural exchange – provided you have something unique to sell. According to UNESCO data, world trade in creative goods and services (covering audio visual, design, music, advertising, computer games, and publishing) totalled a record £400 billion in 2011, doubling the 2002 figure despite the global recession. Cultural ambience also affects tourism. The real danger to Scotland of cultural domination and parochialism lies from staying inside the Union with its dominant Metropolitan culture. Public spending on the arts is heavily skewed toward London. The UK capital benefits to the tune of £69 per head in public subsidies for art and culture, compared with a miserly £4.58 in other English regions. Scotland is in a better position because of decisions taken under devolution, but the concentration of cultural decision-making in London still skews where the major spending goes. In Europe, by contrast, decisions on cultural funding are highly devolved.

## Objection 2: Independent Scotland Could Not Afford Free University Education

The devolution period since 1999 has seen a significant divergence in the education systems of Scotland and the rest of the UK. South of the border the process of dismantling the comprehensive system which began under New Labour has gathered pace with the Conservative-Liberal Democrat coalition elected in 2010. At secondary level, stand-alone and often tacitly selective academy schools and faith schools are replacing the traditional local authority comprehensives. At university level, student tuition fees are now mandatory.

North of the border, the social democratic ethos that infuses the new sense of Scottish national identity has worked to retain the comprehensive approach and free university education. As a result, participation in higher education in Scotland in 2010–11 was an all-time high of 55.6 per cent (of 16–30-year-olds) compared to 47 per cent in England.

Scotland funds free university education from its UK Treasury block grant. It chooses to do so in preference to spending the money elsewhere. There is no reason why it should not go on making that distinct cultural choice. In fact, given the precarious state of UK finances, there is a strong argument for saying that if Scotland wants to keep (never mind evolve) its distinctive culture and education system, then it needs economic independence to fund it. In fact, by deliberately boosting graduate numbers in the economy, Scotland will increase productivity, economic growth and tax revenues proportionately. Contrary to myth, student numbers are increasing significantly in 'hard' subjects. In the period 2001–11, Scottish undergraduate numbers rose by 16 per cent in medicine and 20 per cent in science and engineering subjects.

In the internationally respected QS rankings of universities, conducted on a global basis, Edinburgh University ranks as the 17th best with Glasgow as 51st. That's impressive for a small country – France and Japan only have two universities each in the top 50 QS ratings for 2013, and Germany only one. The QS puts St Andrews University at 83 and Aberdeen at 148, giving Scotland four universities in the top global 200 – a unique resource economically. But in the last resort, the cultural argument for independence is not about economics.

Primarily it is about creating the space for free expression and experiment in the realm of ideas.

## Conclusion

There has been a long debate about lack of self-confidence in Scotland – lack at an individual level and a national level. A survey undertaken by Edinburgh University in 1998, for the World Health Organisation, found that more 11–15-year-olds in Scotland reported low self-confidence compared to their peers in other countries – Scotland ranked 23rd out of 29 industrial countries. So worried was the then Labour administration in the Scottish Parliament that they funded an independent Centre for Confidence and Well-Being, in 2005. Low self-esteem has its roots in Scotland's subordinate status in the Union, in the dominance in the UK of metropolitan culture, and in the lack of opportunity caused by the absence of social mobility in the UK. Independence would be a cultural revolution that lets the Scots rediscover their national and individual self-confidence by removing this perception of being second class. What better way for Scotland's young people to find new opportunities for fulfilment than building a new country?

# EPILOGUE

## *A No Vote Settles Nothing*

Suppose the SNP loses the independence referendum and the constitutional status quo prevails. Game, set and match to the Unionists for the next 30 years? Quite the opposite: for the reality behind the calling of the referendum is the obsolescence of the British state itself, not the political charisma of Alex Salmond. This ramshackle state, designed to run a colonial empire not a modern European democracy, is going to implode anyway, sooner or later. Implode because none of the big three Unionist parties have any plans to reform the UK constitution. They only react to pressure. The title of the referendum No campaign is 'Better Together' but British 'togetherness' is already dead. The 2011 census included an intra-British identity question for the first time. Some 60 per cent of people in England gave their national identity as English 'only' compared to 19 per cent who gave it as British only. Polling by the IPPR think tank shows that identification with English identity is growing. The highest support lies in the North East of England with over 80 per cent of people saying their Englishness comes first. No wonder the pro-Labour New Statesman had a front cover which read: 'Can Miliband speak for England?'

Equally, a No vote will not extinguish Scottish national identity, which is based on unique institutions, a separate culture, and different community values from the rest of the UK. Even if Scotland says No this time, Holyrood still gets to control income tax after 2016 – which must presage eventual Edinburgh control over welfare spending and the economy. A No vote will only postpone the inevitable constitutional breakup of Britain. Unfortunately, it might create political circumstances in which that inevitable breakup is factious. One strong possibility is that an English backlash against the London elite takes Britain out of the EU and sees Westminster dominated by anti-Cameron Tories in actual or tacit alliance with UKIP. Don't imagine that the Barnett Formula (which guarantees Scotland its pro rata share of Westminster public spending increases) would survive. And how many Scots want to live in a UK dominated by the politics of Nigel Farage? A lost independence referendum certainly isn't going to make the SNP disappear. The Nationalists may take a hit but they will roll with the punches. The SNP will still have a majority at Holyrood and probably still be largest party at Holyrood after the 2016 Scottish Parliament elections. That virtually guarantees increased devolution (devo-max), to keep the Nats in their Edinburgh box. After all, devo-max would be a good excuse to reduce the number of Scots MPs. So much for a lost referendum putting the constitutional question into cold storage. It could still see Alex Salmond remain as First Minister at Holyrood but with full fiscal powers.

Meanwhile, in Northern Ireland popular sentiment is coalescing around increased devolution. The Irish Nationalist community sees this as a temporary, halfway house during the economic crisis in the Republic. Pragmatic Unionists see devo-max as the best option given Westminster's perennial lack of interest in the province. Next stop Northern Ireland becomes (effectively) self-governing, then in a generation quietly federates with the Republic.

What of England? Westminster parties have deliberately ignored English domestic political identity since 1945. Win or lose, the Scottish independence referendum – exposed nightly on television – will ignite the fires of English patriotism. There is nothing wrong with that unless the big Westminster parties ignore the need for a separate English Parliament and allow resurgent English nationalism to be captured by the extreme right. When all is said and done, independence for Scotland would be good for England too. She would have to come to terms with herself, embracing the good and excoriating the bad.

In recent polls, six out of ten English people aged 16–44 say they are opposed to or agnostic about Scotland staying in the UK. Support for the United Kingdom is heavily biased by age, with the generation closest to the Second World War the most committed. Demography is undermining the Union surely and steadily. What is fated to emerge from the chrysalis is the four UK nations recovering fiscal and domestic sovereignty then re-establishing some sort of loose, confederal arrangement to manage their common internal market and common security needs. Why are the big three Unionist parties constitutionally myopic? Labour's modern ideological roots are more to do with Stalinist central planning than Christian socialism, and you need a centralist state to issue orders. Now the Stalinist boat has foundered, Labour still needs its Celtic-fringe MPs to have any hope of getting a majority at Westminster – it won only 28 per cent of the English vote in the 2010 General Election. The Lib Dems supposedly favour a UK federal solution but they have never done anything about it, largely because they have never agreed what federalism means. Even this platonic policy stance has been betrayed by Nick Clegg's desire to sit at the Cabinet table. As for the Tories, there is a minimal excuse because constitutional conservatism is their political *raison d'etre*. But the traditional Tory voting base has long since fragmented, white-van man dabbling with the populist, English nationalist right. At some stage, the Tories will have to grasp the need to divorce the Celtic fringes or become a minority party in perpetuity. In 2010, the Conservatives won an overall English majority, with 297 seats to Labour's 191 and the Lib Dem's 43. *Sans* the Celtic fringes, Cameron would have had an overall majority of 61 and no need to form a coalition.

Whatever the outcome, the 2014 Scottish referendum is only a constitutional way-station on the road to the inevitable breakup of the centralist, anti-democratic British state. A Yes vote brings the best chance that a fresh, willing partnership can emerge between the nations of the Atlantic Archipelago. Postponing Scottish independence merely ensures the eventual dissolution of the United Kingdom will take place in more adverse and possibly factious circumstances. Better to embrace the positive now than surrender to our fears, and let negativity triumph.

# PART TWO

# THE CASE FOR NO

# ABOUT THE AUTHOR

Alan Cochrane is Scottish Editor of the *Daily Telegraph*. He began his career with DC Thomson publications in Dundee, Perth and Inverness. He became the Lobby correspondent with the *Mail on Sunday* and *Daily Express* and subsequently worked as a senior executive and columnist with the *Sunday Express*, *Mail on Sunday* and *Sunday Telegraph* on Fleet Street, and with *Scotland on Sunday*, the *Scotsman* and the *Scottish Daily Express* in Scotland. He is married with four children, two of which live in Scotland, two of which live in England, as does his grandson.

# INTRODUCTION

Other than the odd parking ticket and speeding fine, my only serious act of law breaking occurred in 1970. It was then that I perpetrated the heinous crime against the Representation of the People Act by 'voting early and voting often'. What happened was this: I was a young journalist working for the *Courier and Advertiser*'s district office in Perth but I'd happened to be in my native city of Dundee, 22 miles away, to see my girlfriend, and stayed the night at my mother's house. When I awoke it was election day – 18 June 1970 – and I trooped along to the polling station in the local school to cast my vote.

I then hopped on a bus into the city centre and took the train to Perth and it was after dumping my bag at the flat I shared with a couple of colleagues that the 'crime' was committed – because I dropped in on the local polling station and voted AGAIN! Breaches of the above act are liable, on summary conviction, to attract fines of up to £1,000 and as

I had voted twice in two different constituencies there is little doubt that I could have been clobbered.

However, I made no attempt to hide my crime and, indeed, I boasted openly and loudly that I had voted for the same party twice – the party that I had always supported: The Scottish National Party.

At school I was very much the nationalist. I'm not sure if I was ever a party member in the formal sense but I wore an SNP badge in my school blazer – a little red lion on a Saltire background – and my contemporaries would vouch for the fact that in any school debate or mock election I was always the one putting forward the SNP argument.

In my off-duty time, especially during the school holidays when I worked in a butcher's, I took time off between making sausages and mince to write letters to the local paper – that same *Courier* where I eventually got a job as a reporter – espousing the Nationalist cause. Astonishingly, they even printed one.

I wasn't brought up in an overtly Nationalist household, although both parents were sympathetic in the way that many Scots were and – to an extent – still are, in that they moaned about the use of the word 'Britain' when broadcasters meant England and how London tended to be blamed when things went wrong. My father never revealed his politics (at a guess I'd say he was a working-class Tory) but I have little doubt that in the years before he died in 1996 he had decided to vote SNP. My mother came from a strong Labour background, or at least Independent Labour Party background – that was my granny's party, or so she said. But then she seemed to like things with initials like the ILP; being Irish-born and Glasgow Catholic, she also swore allegiance to the IRA on occasion.

And at her knee I was brought up to actively dislike Winston Churchill, who, until 1922, had been MP for Dundee. He was thrown out in favour of the prohibitionist Edward Scrymgeor Wedderburn – Neddy Scrymgeor to his followers. As James Cameron, later one of Britain's most famous journalists and who had, as a young man, spent some time in Dundee looking after his author father, said: 'One of Britain's most alcoholic cities had returned a tee-total, prohibitionist!' But, of course, it was the women who put him in; they'd finally got the vote and his promise to shut the pubs, and prevent their menfolk from drinking what little money the family had, was the clincher.

Still, I digress.

The point is that at this stage I considered myself very much a 'Nat', though, like many young Scots at that time, I have never really spent much time in England.

I finally made it to London – on April Fool's Day, 1974 – and stayed there for 20 years. The Glasgow office of the *Express* had been closed and myself and three others were transferred to Fleet Street.

These were heady days for a twenty-something lad in journalism. Fleet Street was still the street of dreams, the earth moved every night when the mighty presses of all the great newspapers started up sometime after 10 p.m. when the first edition started to roll. And, incredibly, it was Scots who ruled the roost in so many offices. Most papers had an irascible Scot – is there any other kind? – on the News Desk; my own paper, the old broadsheet *Daily Express*, had a Scottish editor.

Politically, it was almost a badge of bravado amongst my many fellow London-Scots to present oneself as a Scottish nationalist and the fact that we were living in the capital city was put down as a temporary phenomenon – we would always go home one day. The truth of this, as it turned out, was somewhat different and most stayed in the south.

In becoming a political correspondent, which I did in 1978, I found it very convenient to suggest, however obliquely, to the mostly Tory and Labour politicians with whom I came into contact that I was a supporter of the SNP. MPs always try to find out the political affiliations of journalists and, in those days, nobody took the SNP very seriously, so to profess sympathy for them was a good way of ingratiating oneself with – or at least not alienating – Tory and Labour politicians.

I covered the first Scottish referendum on what was then called 'Home Rule' in 1979, albeit a very watered down version of the devolution that Scotland eventually achieved 20 years later, and was furious when the ridiculous 40 per cent rule[1] meant that even though a majority voted in favour, the Assembly, as it was then called, wasn't set up.

However, in succeeding years, I suppose my conversion to a British, as distinct from an exclusively Scottish viewpoint, became inexorable. It wasn't until I returned to Scotland in 1994 – on another April Fool's Day – that I realised that it had actually happened. I realised I was (and remain) proud of great British institutions – the Civil Service, the Monarchy, the Armed Forces – oh definitely the Armed Forces – and even the BBC, although of late this has become more difficult. At this point the devolution campaign was in full swing. A Tory administration in Scotland was under fire from all sides for defying what had become, as the late John Smith put it, 'the settled will of the Scottish people'. But from my new perspective it was difficult to escape the conclusion that devolution could only lead one way – towards an increasing demand for complete separation.

As Prime Minister John Major – someone I seldom agree with – said, support for devolution suggested that Scotland was now 'sleepwalking towards independence'. The longer I was back in Scotland, the more I believed that the idea of breaking up Britain made no sense whatsoever. I found it an incredibly dispiriting prospect. Of course I am proud to be Scottish; Scotland has a fantastic history and, for a small country, we have contributed an incredible amount to the world and international affairs. But equally, I know I am an intensely proud Brit. For one thing, the United Kingdom of Great Britain and Northern Ireland is still a major player on the world scene and we are a part of this; for another, the 300-year-old union between Scotland and England is the most successful coming together of two former enemies that the world has ever seen.

◻ ◻ ◻

I give you this background to make the point that my opposition to the proposed separation, as I suspect is the case with many Scots, is not a simple position to take. In fact, while my opposition has remained consistent, there are many aspects of SNP policy that I have supported. In fact I think that, other than independence and education, I have supported more SNP policies than I have opposed.

For instance, I was definitely one of the few – the very few – who supported the freeing of Megrahi, the convicted Lockerbie bomber. I did so because I believed and accepted the medical advice that the Scottish Government received that he was dying from terminal cancer and had no longer than three months to live. It was not an easy decision to support. It put me at serious odds with the official policy of the *Daily Telegraph*, my employer. However, it is massively to its credit – both editor and management – that no attempt was made to get me to change my mind to fall in line with *Telegraph* policy. This belief put me on the opposite side of the argument voiced by the relatives of the victims of that terrorist massacre who said that no mercy was shown to their sons and daughters, and so why should any be shown to their murderer? It was a very difficult point of view to counter. However, I believed that the SNP ministers involved, Kenny McAskill, the justice minister, and Alex Salmond, the First Minister, had acted from the best of motives. Yes, I did have a nagging suspicion at the back of my mind that Alex Salmond may have been grandstanding – it is an easy criticism to level at him – and putting himself on the world's stage in controversial circumstances in the process, but I decided to give him the benefit of the doubt.

However, I also think that where the SNP have been shown to be wholly in the wrong is in not admitting that, because Megrahi lived for two more years and nine months, they had made a mistake in freeing him when they did. To continue to defend the medical opinion that led to his being sent back to Libya, when it was crystal clear that that medical opinion was hopelessly mistaken, was, in my opinion, just plain stupid. And to this day no word of apology has been uttered over Megrahi's release.

Arguments about the 'important' issues, such as the economy, cross-border security, NATO, and EU membership may well dominate the column inches and the airwaves in the run-up to the referendum on independence. Whilst each is vital to the future of Scotland, whether it's in or out of the Union, I believe it is emotion that will play a huge part in the final decision. In spite of our reputation as a dour lot, the Scots are a passionate people and the Nats can be expected to appeal to that personal quality in full measure in 2014. There's the 700th anniversary of the Battle of Bannockburn – arguably the most famous event in this ancient nation's history – in June. And although it was a victory that secured Scottish independence and which should be acknowledged and celebrated by all Scots, there can be little doubt that the SNP will try to hi-jack the anniversary for its own ends. I don't blame them; there's not much else going for them.

Bannockburn is, without doubt, an important historic milestone in my Scottishness but I refuse to see what it's got to do with the present argument about the relationship between Scotland and England. I shall honour the memory of that battle for its own sake, not for its relevance to today's events.

To my mind, two much more significant milestones arrive in August and September 2014 with the 100th and 75th anniversaries, respectively, of the First and Second World Wars. Then the peoples of Britain, together with what were still, certainly in the case of the first conflict, the people of the Empire stood side by side against a common foe. This is not the place to revisit the arguments about the cause of the first global conflict but as regards the events of September 1939, surely Britons can take a joint pride from the fact that this country – that is the United Kingdom of Great Britain and Northern Ireland – stood alone against the Nazi tyranny.

That, much more than a medieval battle, will surely have a greater relevance for voters in this referendum. To be sure there hasn't been an Oscar-winning movie on either the First or Second World Wars to match the likes of Braveheart, which charted, in a wholly fictional – even imaginary – sense, the early years of the Scottish wars of independence. But I find it vastly encouraging that many young people are interested, even in some cases fascinated, by those twentieth-century conflicts and the role of Britain in them. My 16-year-old daughter visited the Somme and Flanders battlefields in a school trip last year and she and her teenage pals were visibly moved, sometimes to tears, by the scenes they witnessed, especially the daily 'Last Post' ceremony at the Menin Gate in Ypres. And on their coach journey home they all joined in the singing of such trench-war classics as 'It's a Long Way to Tipperary' and 'Willie McBride'.

And this leads me to the first area that I would like to look at in more detail: the fundamental question of our identity.

---

*Notes*

1  An amendment to the legislation, ironically tabled by a Scottish MP, who represented a London constituency, ruled that at least 40 per cent of ALL THOSE WHO ACTUALLY VOTED had to vote 'yes' for the assembly to be set up. There was a simple majority in favour of the assembly but the 40 per cent was not reached.

# 1

# IDENTITY

This is one of the most difficult areas to deal with, largely because of the conflicting loyalties held by many Scots. The polls tend to show that, if asked to state their priorities, most would say they were Scottish first and British second but, in my experience, these definitions are very often inter-changeable and dependent on circumstances. For instance, it is by now well documented how many Scots enjoyed being part of a successful British entry in last year's Olympics, and in the run-up to the London Games, they played a full part in the Olympic Torch's progress through Scotland.

With so many Union Jacks being flourished in every corner of Scotland, a clearly infuriated Alex Salmond spent £10,000 of British taxpayers' pounds in hiring hard-up students to dish out hundreds of Scottish Saltire flags, as replacements for the Union Jacks, to bemused bystanders in Edinburgh's Royal Mile as the Torch-bearers approached. Anyone who doubts the levels of pettiness to which this

debate can descend should always be reminded of that epi-
sode.

And in the Games themselves, most Scots cheered as lust-
ily as those from elsewhere in these islands as the gold medals
rolled in, won in a few cases by Scots but mostly, given the
sheer size difference between the countries, by English athletes. And it infuriated most Nats that those Scottish athletes
who were successful insisted that they enjoyed being part of a
British team and that they couldn't have won their respective
events without British support, subsidy and, in many cases,
training facilities.

Prominent in this respect has been Scotland's – and indeed
Britain's – greatest-ever Olympian, Sir Chris Hoy who has
been unashamed and refreshingly forthright in his declaration of his Britishness. And his every success has been greeted
through gritted teeth by most Nats who cannot bear to laud
his success but dare not attack his choice of national affili-
ation. In a country that produces so few sporting heroes as
does Scotland, Hoy simply cannot – and, frankly, should not
– be criticised. Andy Murray is in a similar situation, although
he has managed to escape being trapped by being asked to
state his preference for Scottishness or Britishness. He did,
however, earn the undying enmity of many English people for
joking – and it was a joke – that he'd support anyone who was
playing England in an international competition. This, again,
is a common Scottish trait that is widely deplored south of
the border and also among many Scots; mostly, I'm bound to
conclude, by those who know little of football.

But there is no doubt that it does cause problems for
Scots in England. Most English people cannot under-

stand why, when they would always support the Scottish team against foreign neighbours, the Scots would support England's opposition.

The issue is deemed to be political or even racist. It is neither; it is about football, pure and simple. Take the example of Rangers and Celtic. Fans of the former will normally wish the latter to be defeated, no matter who they're playing – and vice versa - and the same is true as regards great rivals like Manchester United and Manchester City. Scottish football fans regard the English team as their greatest rival and would normally wish to see them defeated. That has been the case for decades, although I've detected what looks like a diminution of this trait in recent years thanks to the woeful state of the Scottish international side. But if our fortunes improve, will the national desire to see the English team be hammered return with a vengeance? Pathetic? Yes, I suppose it is, but then this is often the default position of small countries in relation to their larger neighbours.

One of the strangest stories I have heard in this regard is that told to me by a senior BBC executive, based in Glasgow, who was charged to investigate this anti-English phenomenon just before a World Cup match between England and Germany a decade or more ago. He sent a camera crew to Erskine Hospital where they interviewed a limbless ex-serviceman about his preferences for the match. Now, this man had had his right leg blown off by an Afrika Corps mine in the Libyan desert in 1942 – that's right, an explosive planted by the Germans – but he had no doubt about where his loyalties lay. 'I hope the Krauts hammer the bloody English,' he laughed.

On another occasion, whilst I was editor of the *Scottish Daily Express*, I had arranged for John Jeffrey, the Scottish flank forward, nicknamed the White Shark, to write a rugby column for my newspaper. I drove down to Kelso in the Scottish Borders for dinner with him. He arrived late, beaming all over his face. He was delighted as he told me about trouble at a football match in Ireland: 'The bloody English fans are rioting in Dublin. What a shower they are.'

Now, this was the same JJ (his other nickname) who professed an undying hatred of the English but who counted as one of his closest pals, Brian Moore, the English hooker, with whom he played an impromptu game of street rugby with the Calcutta Cup after a Murrayfield international. The cup was damaged and both men were heavily punished by their respective rugby authorities.

Of course, the one place where the separatists have a decided and visible advantage is on symbols. I am well aware that what were called 'flags and emblems' were and still are a significant and sometimes incendiary part of the recent troubles in Northern Ireland and accept that the issue is not nearly so controversial in Scotland. However, it wrong to ignore the issue altogether.

Largely due to the stupidity of the Unionist camp – and especially its Labour part – Scotland's national flag, the Saltire or St Andrew's Cross, has been corralled, purloined might be a better word, by the SNP. Just as Bannockburn was a Scottish, and not an SNP, triumph, so the Saltire is as much my flag as theirs. To this end, the fobs on both my car and house keys feature Saltires. And I regularly wear a tie that features the St Andrew's Cross. If truth be told I wear it to annoy

– successfully – my Nationalist friends because it has nothing to do with any sympathy I may have for their cause; it is in fact the tie of the Caledonian Club of London, of which I've been a member, on and off, for some 30 years.

By and large, SNP supporters make a lot more noise about their cause than do their opponents and can turn out for rallies and marches at the drop of a hat, brandishing, of course, all those Saltires. Those who oppose separation tend to be an altogether more subdued group, or at least thus far. While they might work together happily enough in the Better Together campaign, it's difficult to imagine Tory, Labour and Liberal Democrat activists taking to the streets to Save the Union. It's difficult, too, to imagine them brandishing hundreds of Union Jacks, which is a pity. Unfortunately, that flag appears to be associated too closely with the UK's far-Right political groupings, such as the National Front or British National Party. The SNP hate the Union Jack; to them it's the Butcher's Apron, but I believe a determined bid should be made to recapture both flags for the Unionist cause. They are not the exclusive property of any political party or cause, nor should they be.

Perhaps the most important symbol, or should I say institution, that will be affected by independence is the monarchy and it is on this issue that I find the nationalists' hypocrisy quite frankly breathtaking. Alex Salmond and the leadership have made sure that the SNP's official policy is for the Queen to remain Head of State of an independent Scotland. Initially, the plan was to have the Presiding Officer of the Scottish Parliament as Head of State unless and until a referendum was held on the future of the monarchy.

Now the plan is to repeal the Act of Union of the Parliaments, which occurred in 1707, but to honour the Union of the Crowns, which occurred more than a century earlier in 1603 when James VI succeeded Elizabeth I and became James I of England and Great Britain. Now, I don't ever remember the SNP conference – that party's supreme policy making body – debating that issue. However, they insist it has been properly discussed so I can only assume – given that I've attended every one of their annual get-togethers for the last 20 years and a few before that – that I must have nipped out for a fag or a pee when they reached that momentous decision. And it is momentous for the simple reason that the majority of SNP members and activists are out-and-out republicans or at very least support the idea of an immediate referendum on whether or not the monarchy should continue in 'their' new Scotland. And although the Yes campaign is, nominally, an amalgam of various pro-independence forces, it is dominated by the SNP. This has generated several ripples, if not ructions, in the ranks, with Patrick Harvie, the Greens leader, disagreeing openly with the SNP policy agenda. And the issue of the monarchy has caused serious divisions. Dennis Canavan, the former Scottish Labour MP and ex-independent MSP, is now co-chair of Yes and he has openly disagreed with Mr Salmond over the Queen remaining Head of State. He says there must be a referendum on whether the House of Windsor should continue to provide Scotland's Heads of State.

For reasons of not scaring the horses – a maxim that seems to guide much of what he says and does – Alex Salmond brooks no internal discussion within his party on the monarchy and personally he evinces what appears to be a genuine respect and liking for Queen Elizabeth II. He is not unusual in that respect; almost every politician who's ever had to deal with the Queen has fallen under the same spell. Interestingly, however, Elizabeth Windsor's very title grates enormously with older and more fundamentalist nationalists. She is not Elizabeth II of Scotland, only of England and when pillar boxes with the insignia 'ERII' were first erected in the 1950s, after she was raised to the throne, they were blown up by angry nationalists. It is just about the only evidence that Scottish separatists were prepared to resort to the bomb, rather than the ballot box. There is even a once-popular folk-song about the issue which goes: 'Nae Liz the One, nae Lizabeth the Twa, Nae Liz will ever dae. We will mak oor land republican in the Scottish breakaway.' Mind you, I suspect that if anyone was to be caught singing it nowadays at an SNP official function, they'd be slung out of the party straightaway.

Mr Salmond and the Queen meet reasonably often when she stays at the Palace of Holyroodhouse in Edinburgh and he and his wife, Moira, are annual overnight guests at Balmoral, the Royal Family's Highland residence. That is an honour – although Tony Blair's wife, Cherie, regarded it as a tiresome chore – that he shares on an equal basis with the British Prime Minister.

Because of all politicians' strict adherence to Royal protocol, we are never permitted to know what they discuss with the Head of State, although it is a 'given' that the Queen is always fantastically well briefed on what's happening in every part of her kingdom(s). But, thanks to both the

Queen's and First Minister's avid interest in horse-racing – Mr Salmond is a sometime newspaper tipster – it is probably safe to assume that horse flesh might figure highly on their list of conversations.

But what does the Queen think of Mr Salmond's plan to make her Queen of Scots? (Historically Scotland's monarchs have been Kings or Queens of the people, not the land mass). Mr Salmond can't, or won't, tell us if he's persuaded Her Majesty to accept this change of title or even if he's mentioned it to her and, needless to say, there has been a deafening silence from Buckingham Palace and Her Majesty's advisors on the issue. But I have absolutely no doubt that she and they will have formed an opinion on whether she wants this new title. Both the Queen and Prince of Wales, who spends a great deal of time in Scotland where his working title is Duke of Rothesay, have consulted widely with several SNP and opposition ministers. For instance, a number of senior nationalists, as well as Mr Salmond, have been guests at Birkhall, Charles and Camilla's home on the Balmoral Estate. These have included John Swinney, the influential Scottish finance minister and former SNP leader, and – interestingly because she is an avowed republican – Roseanna Cunningham. After much idle chit-chat, and perhaps not a little malt whisky, I understand that invariably Prince Charles turns the conversation round to weightier matters. 'And what', I can imagine he might ask, 'would you think might be the role of the Family, if Scotland were to become independent?'

As we might expect, the Queen has a wide circle of advisors, official and unofficial, in Scotland. One of her senior ladies-in-waiting is Ginny, Countess of Airlie, whose husband

David, is the Earl of Airlie and a former Lord Chamberlain and, as such, head of Her Majesty's household. The late Michael Shea was formerly her press secretary at Buckingham Palace and, until his untimely death, was an extremely well-connected pillar of the Edinburgh and Scottish establishment. The Earl of Dalhousie, a near-neighbour to the Royal estates in the North East of Scotland is also a leading light in the Royal Company of Archers, Her Majesty's Bodyguard in Scotland. And as someone who is reputed to be a stickler for protocol, the Queen can also call on advice from the Knights of the Thistle, Scotland's highest order of chivalry, and whose ranks include Lord (George) Robertson of Port Ellon, a former NATO Secretary General, UK Defence Secretary and shadow Scottish Secretary, and Lord (David) Steel of Aikwood, former leader of the Liberal Democrats and first presiding officer of the Scottish Parliament. Both are staunch Unionists.

However, as a constitutional monarch, the Queen's principal advisor is the Prime Minister of the United Kingdom of Great Britain and Northern Ireland and acts at all times in consultation with him (or her). It is difficult to imagine that she has not discussed the independence issue with David Cameron, or for that matter with other UK ministers and indeed – as head of the Commonwealth – other leaders of countries where she is Head of State.

Equally, will she not have asked Alex Salmond about his plans? I can't believe that she hasn't raised the subject.

At the back of all nationalist minds, I'm sure, is a sneaking fear that the Queen might intervene in the independence debate. She did so in the run up to the 1979 referendum when she was reported as saying that she was very aware that she was Queen of a United Kingdom. This was seen – correctly in my view – as an expression of opposition to the then more modest plans for a devolved parliament. It was an extraordinary intervention by a constitutional monarch. The difference this time is Alex Salmond plans something much more dramatic – the very break up of the United Kingdom and the abolition of the entity that's become known as Great Britain. Will she speak out in the coming months? Or has Mr Salmond's offer to make her Queen of Scots satisfied her that she and her successors will retain their constitutional role in this new entity? I would hope that she makes her views known before the referendum. Indeed, I think her subjects deserve no less.

However, we now get a whole series of entirely specious arguments about Scottish identity from the separatists. At its root is the view that the Scots are somehow vastly different but also completely superior to their English neighbours. At one level it suggests that the Scots, almost alone in these islands, support the maintenance of the Welfare State as originally constituted. At its worst, as exemplified during a programme hosted by the former Rt Revd Richard Holloway that I heard recently, it posited that only the Scots stood firm against what the programme said was Margaret Thatcher's dismantling of the Welfare State and the imposition of the Community Charge, better known as the Poll Tax. No acknowledgment was made of the fact that the latter was opposed in every corner of the United Kingdom; indeed from within the Cabinet and Conservative Party it actually formed the basis of Michael Heseltine's campaign against Thatcher. And it was the anti-poll-tax riot in Trafalgar Square that finally convinced the then Tory government that the measure was doomed.

Equally, no front line Nat accepts that changes in our benefits' system were opposed all over the United Kingdom. The Nats and their arrogant fellow travellers insist that it's only the Scots, with their allegedly superior social consciences, who are prepared to stand up for the disadvantaged in our midst. It is nonsense and, frankly, it borders on racist nonsense.

Other than the horrible 'here's tae us, wha's like us' maxim that still attracts many Scots, I cannot understand from whence this egotistical stance emanates. Can it be that few Scots know anyone who lives in the rest of the UK? Have they never met people of a similar background to themselves from England, Wales or Northern Ireland? I do think that this is part of the trouble, as I'm completely astounded by how few people I know – especially journalists and young journalists – who never, well hardly ever, visit the rest of the UK. Is that the reason for their ignorance of the views of people elsewhere? Or do they think that everyone in England went to Eton or another public school and is well-off?

This continuing striving to prove that we Scots are totally different from the English is, I find, very depressing. It is allied to the view that bad things are 'done' to the Scots by the English, which harks back to my earlier argument that there is no recognition amongst most Nats that Scots are as much the authors of Britishness as are the English and if British governments have pursued policies of which some Scots disapprove, then it is an issue of politics, not nationality. I heard a ludicrous argument recently that suggested that it was the

UCS shipyard sit-in that first turned Scots against the idea of Britishness and then that was confirmed a decade or so later with the closure of Ravenscraig. No evidence is presented to back up these views, however; just as with many separatist policies, it appears that it will suffice to take an assertion and repeat it as often as possible until it takes root.

But the dark side of this position is the emergence of what can only be described as a new racism.

While I would of course agree that the majority of SNP members are not prejudiced against English people *per se*, equally I have absolutely no doubt that many people who support breaking up Britain are indeed racist, in that they actively dislike, if not hate, the English. Scottish police forces report an increase in assaults which have an anti-English motive and, whilst the figures are disputed, I would believe that most English people living in Scotland would attest to having been the recipient of casual but frequent abuse on account of their nationality. Being called 'an English bastard' is, sadly, far from uncommon.

# 2

# BORDERS AND IMMIGRATION

The SNP claim that what they call the 'social union' between Scotland, England, Wales and Northern Ireland would be maintained. There would be no borders or border controls so there would be complete freedom of movement between the constituent parts of what we currently call the United Kingdom of Great Britain and Northern Ireland.

This is extremely far-fetched and unlikely. The nationalists say that they would have a much freer immigration policy than is currently being proposed by the Coalition Government at Westminster. If this came to pass it is difficult to imagine that England would permit an open and porous border whereby immigrants, having been admitted without let or hindrance to Scotland, could then travel freely into England.

Immigration has become a huge and contentious political issue in England, with the Tories trying desperately to stem the flow and former Labour Cabinet ministers admitting, shamefacedly, that they allowed far too many migrants into this country and underestimated the effect their presence would have on the native community. David Blunkett, the former Home Secretary, has been especially vocal in decrying the effect the large Roma influx is having on his native city of Sheffield and its inhabitants. Depressingly, the greatest tension appears to be between newly arrived Roma and second- and third-generation families from the Indian subcontinent. The latter claim that the Roma 'don't understand the British way of life'.

Scotland, on the other hand, is arguably the European country least affected by immigration. There are tiny numbers here; the most dense being a sizeable number of Asian families – mostly from Pakistan – in the south side of Glasgow. They are pretty well integrated and play a very full part in both the public and business life of the city and country – with councillors and members of both the UK and Scottish Parliaments, as well as a great many successful businessmen, coming from their midst. But elsewhere in Scotland the numbers of immigrants is miniscule.

The SNP believe that they must have a greater influx of immigrants if they're to achieve the economic growth they have been targeting. And they might well be right. But if they do this and have what would be an 'open border' policy they must be alive to the possibility that many immigrants would use their unrestricted entry to Scotland to move quickly into England where, for instance, they may already have families, friends or communities of the same ethnic background. Thus, there is no chance whatsoever that the authorities in the rest of the UK would do anything other than set up some form of Immigration Control at the main border crossing points. The political pressure on them to do so would be intense and, frankly, overwhelming. Incidentally, as there is a huge number of road and rail routes which currently cross the border between England and Scotland might we see a significant reduction in these to better facilitate controls?

There is also a lot of stunning hypocrisy from the nationalist leadership about immigration and Scots' reaction to it. Too many prominent Scots decry the attitude of people south of the border to immigration. But they do so with absolutely no inkling of the situation in many parts of England where large numbers of immigrants have arrived over the decades and who now dominate several communities. The idea that Scots are any less racist than their English counterparts is just so much rubbish – as asylum seekers dumped on multi-storey flats in Glasgow would testify. My own view is that, in general terms, Scottish people are neither more nor less anti-immigrant than any other people in these islands. And a recent opinion poll suggested that only 2 per cent of Scots believed in a more liberal immigration policy, proving that Scots have roughly the same loves and hates as their English neighbours.

And, frankly, that opinion extends to just about every other aspect of life, too.

Also on the issue of probable border controls, the SNP is likely to set its own tax and duty rates for alcohol, tobacco and luxury goods which might be markedly different from those in England. In such a situation are we not pretty certain to see Customs officers at ports of entry asking Scots and English travellers the age old question, 'Have you anything to declare?'

Under existing EU rules, new member states have to join Shengen – the free travel across Europe agreement – of which the UK currently has an opt out. If Scotland does join Shengen and the rest of the UK remains out of it, that's another reason why there will have to be border posts between Scotland and England and, of course, between Scotland and Northern Ireland.

So with distinct policies on immigration, asylum-seeking, on rates of duty for alcohol and tobacco, and a different approach to Shengen, there would have be a multiplicity of border checkpoints. In as small an island as this, and a Union as old as this, it would be bonkers. And something that I reckon most Scots would deplore.

# 3

# DEFENCE

It is impossible to speak of the border question without looking at what shape a nation's defence policy might be. The policy objectives outlined in what the Scottish Government called a White Paper but which was, in reality, an SNP political manifesto and should not have been drawn up by supposedly impartial civil servants, is a wish list. And to my mind one of the least defensible of its hopes is, strangely enough, defence. The plans outlined by Angus Robertson, who combines being the party's Westminster leader with being its defence spokesman and campaign director are simply not tenable for a country like Scotland that aims to become a full and active member of NATO. First things first; an independent Scotland under an SNP government would expel UK's nuclear deterrent, housed in the fleet of Trident submarines and based at Faslane on the Clyde, from Scotland.

The Nats say they will negotiate a safe and orderly transfer of these missiles, their submarines and the missiles' stockpile at nearby Coulport, within the lifetime of a 4-year parliament. Although this is a more sensible arrangement than the immediate expulsion, which more militant nationalists have long advocated, it is still an incredibly naïve view to imagine that the rest of the NATO alliance members would countenance such a move from an applicant member. NATO is a nuclear alliance; it is true that only 3 members – the USA, the UK and France possess nuclear weapons – but the rest of the 28 members accept what is known as the alliance's 'nuclear umbrella' and remember NATO's possession of nukes is in no way passive; it has never denied that it is a 'first strike' alliance – in other words it would not hesitate to go nuclear if it thought it necessary. It is a policy like this that makes the SNP's policy so hypocritical. Two of their MSPs resigned the party whip in protest at the conference decision to join NATO. They were the most honest ones.

Other aspects of current NATO policy would make many SNP activists quake with distaste. For instance, two of their 'hero' nations – Denmark and Norway – have been incredibly active in 'out-of-area' NATO operations, including Afghanistan, where the Danes have been one of the more enthusiastic supporters of the war against Taliban insurgency. And both Danish and Norwegian pilots played a leading role in attacking Gadaffi's forces in Libya and helping to topple that dictatorship. Such activities by NATO forces are the sort of actions that the Nats deplore; we should never forget Alex Salmond's deploring of the NATO action against Serbian forces in Kosovo as 'unpardonable folly'.

NATO is not the only hole in the SNP's plan for the defence of an independent Scotland – far from it. It is an incredible mish-mash of wishing and hoping and, frankly, far-fetched nonsense. The SNP state that in an independent Scotland the famous Scottish infantry regiments would be re-established to their pre-Hammond strength and transferred to a new Scottish Army.

This incredible statement assumes that all of the officers, NCOs and men would agree to leave the British Army of which they and their predecessors have been proud members for centuries and move *en masse* to something entirely new and which would have no relationship whatsoever, certainly in the short to medium term, with their former comrades-in-arms in the British Army or their counterparts from other NATO countries.

For those steeped in the traditions of Britain's armed forces, and with the security of the nation uppermost in their minds, the number of troops, submarines, warships and fast jets and other military impedimenta Scotland might possess after independence is all-important.

The SNP says that, as well as all the current Scottish servicemen immediately transferring to the putative Scottish Army, an independent Scotland would also be entitled to share – perhaps one tenth – of the UK's current complement of fast jets, transport aircraft, helicopters, trainers, as well as frigates, destroyers, minesweepers, coastal craft, motor launches, etc.

But, in relation to aircraft, all NATO countries are expected to be able to maintain their own air defence. To this end, nations like Norway and Denmark – again those countries that the SNP professes to admire beyond all others – have invested in approximately 40 fast jets. Currently these are

American-built F16s but both countries are in the process of re-equipping with F35s at around £100 million each. The RAF, too, is to have these expensive planes, to complement its squadrons of Typhoons – but in total no more than 40 or 50 planes. Even if an independent Scotland could negotiate a tenth of this air-fleet, what good would 4 or 5 fast jets be in providing the air defence for Scotland?

The Nats also claim that Scotland contributes more to the UK's defence budget than it gets in return – that is, in defence spending within Scotland. This is a wholly specious argument in that defence spending is not allocated in relation to how much is spent, individually, on the component parts of the United Kingdom – so much for England, so much for Scotland and so on. The United Kingdom as a whole is defended by our Armed Forces; the defence budget is indivisible in the way the nationalists pretend. But then this is just another example of their 'Project Fib'; they'll say anything to prove that they're getting a raw deal from the UK government.

Even more ridiculous is their claim that their planned £2.5 billion annual defence budget would be more than capable of providing all of Scotland's defence requirements. As Auslan Cramb reported in the *Telegraph*, one of Scotland's most senior military figures warned recently that independence would, in fact, leave the country 'inadequately protected' and the rest of the UK 'less well defended' than it is today:

Lt General Sir Alistair Irwin, a former Adjutant General of the British Army, said the SNP's defence budget looked 'a great deal more than a little light', and the break-up of the UK would weaken armed forces north and south of the border.

In a conference last year he also raised doubts over the number of senior officers who would be willing to 'throw over their current careers to take their chances north of the border'.

He added: 'It would be a big assumption to make that every single member of each of the units allocated to the Scottish forces would elect to transfer from the British Army that they had joined, not least because many of them are not themselves Scots. It would be an equally big assumption to make that Scots serving in the navy, in the rest of the army and in the air force would themselves elect to transfer. In fact, there are strong indications to the contrary.'

He also questioned the ability of a Scottish force to recruit the estimated 1,500 people a year it would need to maintain its strength, and doubted whether recruits would want to join a force 'that may not be deployed to do interesting things' and which offered fewer opportunities for serving away from home.

The retired officer told the international conference on Global Security and the Future of Scotland at Glasgow University that in theory it should not be too difficult to agree to the transfer of naval, land and air forces, including regimental names, to a new Scottish Defence Force.

But he questioned whether the Scottish Government understood the 'inherently complex and multi-layered' structure that would have to be put in place to support it.

He also warned that extracting Scottish units and men and women from the three services would deal 'a very significant blow to the defence capability of the rest of the UK'.

He added: 'The result of a split, in my military opinion, would be a British Isles collectively less well defended and whose global interest would be much less well served than they are now'.

He added that whatever the nature of a Scottish force, in defence terms there were a host of reasons, including intelligence and diplomatic assets, why 'we are far better as we are'. Gen Irwin told his audience that even a 'lean' Scottish defence ministry would require significant numbers of civil servants and military men.

He also warned that a proposed army comprising two brigades with units capable of overseas intervention would not be able to sustain such operations at much more than a single battalion level, and would not be sufficient to provide the seed corn needed for special forces.

The plan for a defence force HQ in Faslane on the Clyde would leave it inconveniently distant from government, and none of the three armed services would have training establishments in Scotland.

He said there were precedents for foreign countries sending cadets to the UK, but he had never heard of an entire officer cadet cohort being trained outside its own country.

In addition, career opportunities would be very limited in a small Scottish force, which could cause the organisation to 'atrophy and lose its sparkle', and lead to an 'ageing and less and less agile and capable force'.

(*Telegraph*, 8 November 2013)

# 4

# ECONOMY

But whilst these considerations should weigh heavily with all of those due to vote in next September's referendum, even more pertinent will be the effect that the questions over defence policy have on Scotland's economy and, as a result, on everyone's standard of living.

It was thus vital that Philip Hammond recently spelled out the plain facts of how the defence plans will, I believe, pose a significant and possibly devastating threat to jobs in our defence industries.

The Defence Secretary said that employment in our shipyards and in defence-related industries, as well as at giant bases like Faslane and Coulport, could not be sustained in a separate Scotland with the SNP's proposals for cut-price defence forces.

Mr Hammond's warning was timely and, as his speech in Edinburgh made plain, it is time for employers in the defence industry to explain to their workers that breaking

up Britain and its defence infrastructure would be bad
news for jobs. Union leaders are already saying as much.
Personally I think it's time for the bosses to join them in
speaking out.

Which raises the question of candour and courage in
certain sectors. If I said I was frustrated by the lack of this
from some sections of Scottish opinion about their position
on independence I would be lying: I am absolutely bloody
furious that the business and commercial community have
remained so steadfastly silent about what they think would
be the effect independence might have on their enterprises.
I would exclude only two people from this condemnation;
Iain MacMillian, director of the CBI in Scotland, and Rupert
Soames, CEO of Aggreko. The former has been courageous
in speaking out against the separatists' plans and has been
roundly and publicly condemned by the SNP leadership for
his pains. From where I stand, he appears to have received
precious little support from the companies who are members
of the CBI in Scotland; the result being that his voice has been
all but silenced publicly. The latter, on the other hand, and as
befits a grandson of Winston Churchill, has been resolute in
his criticism of the nationalists and their proposals, insisting
that breaking up the UK would have a hugely detrimental
effect on his business and on business generally. He has said
so publicly, both in addresses to conferences held within
the confines of the Scottish Parliament and in evidence to
a House of Lords committee of inquiry. More than that, Mr
Soames has also appeared to cast a shadow on the nationalist
cause by revealing that many businessmen in Scotland, who
are known to him, are frightened to speak out in support of

the Union because they fear retribution from the SNP and the SNP-run Scottish Government.

From personal knowledge I know this to be true. Businessmen, large and small, have told me that if they've ever so much as suggested that independence might not be a good idea they have been telephoned, and advised that their comments have been deemed 'unhelpful'. With many of them depending on public-sector contracts to help their businesses flourish, they've quickly come to the conclusion that it would be best to keep quiet. This message has been relayed to me and to many others in the anti-independence camp on any number of occasions, where businessmen are happy to tell tales of intimidation but only if their names remain unknown. Interestingly, some have insisted that the time is coming fast when they will speak out publicly against independence; at time of writing I haven't noticed many doing so.

I am pleased to report, however, that in early December the dam was breached, in that three of the four major supermarket giants launched a pre-emptive strike against independence, or at least put a few home truths out there of which people who might be tempted to vote Yes should be aware. Interestingly, only two of the four retailers – ASDA and Morrison – agreed to be quoted in the front-page *Financial Times* story. Their warning was that independence would lead to Scotland being treated, as the nationalists presumably wish, as a complete separate country outside of the UK and, as a result, the higher transport costs of trading in Scotland would no longer be absorbed by British companies.

Morrisons' chief executive Dalton Philips feared that the regulatory environment – red tape, in other words – would change in an independent country and the increased costs would have to be passed on to the ordinary shopper. 'Why should the English and Welsh consumer subsidise this increased cost of doing business in Scotland?' Why indeed. ASDA's chief executive, Andy Clarke, pointed out that, at present, the price of a loaf of bread and a pint of milk is the same across the UK, before adding: 'But the cost of doing business in different parts of the country does vary.'

Sad to say, a day later Morrisons hoisted the white flag of abject surrender and said that whilst they may well have said that prices would be go up after independence, it might also be the case that they could go down ... It had all the air of someone having been got at – possibly in the shape of a wee phone call asking whether they were sure that Morrisons wanted to be part of the problem for SNP supporters. I am not saying that this happened, but it was a very, very hasty retreat.

There is a pointer, perhaps, in the behaviour of these retail bosses for other businessmen in that there may well be safety in numbers. It is just about understandable that small to medium-sized businesses, especially those largely dependent on Scottish Government contracts, keep shtum for fear of losing customers and orders. And even larger concerns lay themselves open to being targeted by those who object to business getting involved in the referendum battle. But banding together, or at least making sure that if you do speak out you're not alone in doing so, appears to offer a bit of security.

One who has spoken out but who has also since retreated has been Maitland Mackie, non-executive chairman of the hugely successful North East ice-cream and potato crisps combine. But he had to retreat quickly after his children, who now run the firm, discovered that their web-site had been attacked and disrupted following Mr Mackie's criticism of independence. He hasn't said much since.

It goes without saying that any intimidating behaviour of this nature is not only outrageous but also, surely, unprecedented and unconstitutional. But with none, or hardly any, of the victims prepared to stand up and be counted, there is no proof, nor anything that can be done about it. Proof, of a sort but sadly at one remove and not admissible as evidence, has come from Robert Peston, the BBC's highly respected business editor. However, Peston's reputation speaks for itself and in a recent online contribution he told the tale of how the boss of very big 'Footsie' company had been having a reasonably well-ordered and business-like meeting with representatives of the Scottish Government. Well-ordered and business-like, that is, until the Chief Executive raised the issue of independence and suggested that it might cause problems for companies like his. At this, Peston reports that the company boss says he found that the mood of the meeting suddenly became 'very dark' and his hosts became 'very aggressive'. This is not an isolated example; many businessmen say much the same about their experience with representatives of the SNP or Scottish Government, which nowadays is one and the same.

This lack of public opposition from the business community does, of course, mask a deep-seated antipathy towards the SNP and also probably underestimates what we know of the total number of people opposed to separation and who will vote 'No' in the referendum.

On the financial side, I've been told from a number of sources that whilst silence from the business community appears to be endemic, some are quite happy to put their hands in their pockets – or into their companies' coffers – to help the cause. Better Together have been reasonably successful in raising money to fight off independence but if there's one concern it is that quite large sums have been pledged to BT but only for delivery closer to the date of the referendum. Lots of businessmen want to see which way the wind's blowing before they part with their cash and one of the problems BT has discovered is that the continuing opposition to independence, as illustrated by the many opinion polls, is hampering their fundraising.

Still, having said that, impressive sums are still being garnered. One private house party in Edinburgh's Georgian New Town managed to hoover up a staggering £47,000 for Better Together from its guests and a dinner in the same neighbourhood did even better again, pulling in £60,000. It's almost certain that much of this cash came from well-heeled businessmen spending their own, rather than their companies' money. However, it's their voices we want, as well as their dosh!

If the business community has been quiet, the higher education sector has been as silent as the grave on the issue of independence. That is a community struck dumb by fear of what will happen if they speak out for the simple reason that they are wholly dependent on the Scottish Government and its education department for its funding. The principals of most of Scotland's ancient and most venerable universities have said nothing about how they think a Yes vote will impact on their seats of learning. They fear everything; a separatist victory, whereby the SNP will have *carte blanche* to do whatever it likes with its universities; but they are also concerned about a success for the No vote and then an SNP victory in the subsequent 2016 Scottish Parliament elections, where the Nats could get their revenge on all those educationalists who opposed them.

In this general denunciation I should, of course, say that there have been notable exceptions to the examples of cowardice. Top of the list of honour is Professor Chris Whatley, vice principal of Dundee University. He earned the not inconsiderable wrath of the Scottish Government in general and of Shona Robison, his local MSP and Sports Minister, when he voiced support for the Better Together campaign. Thankfully, after a great hue and cry in the press, he was immediately supported by three eminent, but sadly recently retired, academics. They were: Emeritus Professor Susan Shaw, former deputy and vice principal of Strathclyde University; Professor High Pennington, Emeritus Professor of Aberdeen University; and Emeritus Professor Ronald J. Roberts of Stirling University. I am pleased to say that their action in writing an open letter was quickly followed by a letter to all of her academic staff from Professor Louise Richardson, the principal and vice chancellor of St Andrew's University. In a defiant gesture, which is bound to earn her the undying enmity of the less-forgiving Nats, but which underlines that university's independence both financially and intellectually from the stultifying educational atmosphere now abroad in Scotland, she urged them to speak out. She said she didn't mind which side of the argument they chose to support but added that any pressure on them to shut up would stop at her door. Bravo.

Obviously the economy is the issue that appears to dominate the referendum battlefield, or at least as far as the main protagonists are concerned. They and their teams put an enormous amount of effort into 'proving' their case; the separatists insisting that Scotland would be a hugely successful country, economically, if it was independent, whilst the Unionists say that while of course Scotland could go it alone, the figures simply do not add up to creating success, in the terms suggested by the Nats.

However, I wonder sometimes whether all those huge numbers being bandied about really get through to the majority of ordinary voters. In this I am probably underestimating the ability of the man and woman in the street to get to grips with such astronomical figures and, if so, it is simply because I have great trouble getting to grips with all those millions and billions myself.

Where they and I both understand perfectly the numbers involved are on the bread and butter issues, especially pensions and also, of course, the price of bread and butter.

On pensions, the Institute of Chartered Accountants of Scotland, as well as other independent analysts, have warned that occupational pensions face real threats once you insert new national boundaries. Pension funds are permitted to continue with shortfalls as long as they're contained within a national boundary but under EU rules those shortfalls or holes must be made good if the funds operate across borders – something that could cost the funds literally millions.

And now we have supermarket chiefs warning that checkout prices would rise after independence, if, as seems likely, the extra transport costs of operating in Scotland are passed on to the consumer. Different rules and regulations relating to supermarkets may also add to companies' costs, which again would be passed on to shoppers. There is also the large supermarket tax that the SNP government imposed, albeit disguised as a health tax, which infuriated the multiples and which may well be responsible for their hard-line attitude towards independence.

The SNP leaders insist that, in spite of breaking away, Scotland and the Scots would be very good friends and neighbours – in fact they say the relationship might even be enhanced as current causes of friction, for instance over public spending rates, would be removed. Business and commerce would be unchanged, they say, as the four parts of what is now the UK would continue to be each other's best customer.

But the fact remains and from which the nationalists cannot escape – indeed in private they boast about it – is that they are creating a situation whereby we shall all live in different countries from those that we currently inhabit. The nationalists should not, in all honesty, dispute that essential fact.

For a long time the English have been apathetic about Scottish independence, their predominant attitude probably best summed by the following statement: 'If you want to go, for God's sake go. But please don't make too much noise about it.' However, there has also been a more hostile attitude, amongst a sizeable minority of English people, to the effect that they believe the Scots have 'sponged' off them –

their words not mine – long enough and that England would be better off without their near neighbour. This has been illustrated by the claim – disputed by the nationalists – that per capita public spending in Scotland is much higher north of the border than south.

In large part any English animus towards the Scots has, in my opinion, has been brought on by the continual public moaning by many Scots about 'perfidious Albion', about how everything that's gone wrong in Scotland is because of the English or at least is caused by London governments. Personally, I've been pleased to see that attitude diminish of late, thanks to a concerted effort by the leaders of the main British parties, David Cameron, Nick Clegg and Ed Miliband, who have extolled the virtues of staying together and who've been happy to attack the nationalists' assertions.

In one specific area, this is highly significant. By this I mean the fact that were it not for the scores of Labour MPs elected in Scotland at every general election, the Conservatives could look forward to winning all the time. But Cameron has said that this electoral bonus is a secondary consideration and that he puts retaining the Union at the top of his political agenda. As well he might; he does not wish to go down in history as the Prime Minister – and Tory Prime Minister at that – who presided over the end of Great Britain and the breakup of the United Kingdom.

All of that said, whatever goodwill might have been engendered by the leaders' efforts were undermined by the assertions from the SNP that they would keep the pound sterling in a currency union with the rest of the UK.

The staggering inability of the SNP to react sensibly when these assertions – disguised as policies – were challenged is a continuing mystery to this observer. The Nats came a cropper on EU membership when their previous position of 'we won't have to apply to join because we will continue to be members of the EU' was rubbished by all and sundry. They were eventually forced to admit that an independent Scotland would have to apply but insisted that they would be fast-tracked, because there would be no opposition to them joining. Even here, there have been repeated warnings – not least from the Spanish, who have their own problem with 'splitters' – that things might not go all that smoothly.

And the biggest reverse came, predictably, on the question of the demand for a sterling currency union with what would be left of the United Kingdom. The SNP position is that because the assertion – that word again – that they'd keep the pound in a currency union was stated in their White Paper on Scottish Independence, it assumed almost-gospel like qualities and could not be gainsaid.

But that's precisely what did happen when, in a ferocious strike, all the economic spokesmen for the three main UK parties – one, or even two, of which will form the British government after next year's general election – said that they could not see circumstances in which an independent Scotland could keep the pound in a currency union. The unprecedented joint action by George Osborne, Danny Alexander and Ed Balls followed the equally unprecedented publication of an analysis conducted by Sir Nicholas Macpherson, the permanent secretary at the Treasury, which concluded that a currency union was 'fraught with difficulty' as it would require not just an extraordinary commitment by both sides, but also a closer union between the peoples involved. And this commitment is unlikely to happen if Scotland votes to, effectively, bring an end to the UK.

What did we get in return from Alex Salmond? A detailed counter-stroke, full of well-worked-out rebuttals? Not this time. In what appeared a foot-stamping response, the best the SNP leader could come up with was to attack what he called the 'bluff, bluster and bullying' of the three UK parties; that and a determination to continue with his assertion – that word again – that an independent Scotland would join a currency union, no matter what the Westminster politicians said.

He repeated his extraordinary claim that he – and not Messrs Osborne, Balls and Alexander, not to mention the First Minister of Wales, who's also opposed to Scotland sharing the pound – knew what was best for the people of England, Wales and Northern Ireland. He also maintained that the businessmen of rUK (the new shorthand for a Scotlandless Union) would support his demand for Scotland to be part of a currency union, as they wouldn't have to pay transaction costs. However, that claim has been well and truly dismissed by the Treasury who've pointed out that, with much bigger trade between Britain and the EU, which uses the euro, and the USA, which uses the dollar, home-based companies cope perfectly well with the transaction costs in those areas.

And the idea that the English, Welsh and Northern Irish would be well-disposed to take a benign and generous attitude towards an independent Scotland – as is Mr Salmond's ever-hopeful case – must now be in serious doubt. That arises because of the SNP's current determination to continue to charge students from these UK regions up to £36,000 each if they decide to come to Scottish universities after independence. At present all EU students must be given free tuition in Scotland, to keep them in line with Scottish students. But rUK students can be charged fees as *discrimination within* member states is permitted. However, if Scotland becomes independent and a separate member of the EU, wouldn't it have to extend free tuition to the English, Welsh and Northern Irish? That's what EU law says, but it's not what the SNP says; they claim that Scotland is a special case and say they'd continue to discriminate against the Brits by making them pay. How's that for making friends and influencing people?

Why would an attitude like that induce Scotland's neighbours to say: 'Oh sure, come and share our pound and have our Bank act as your lender of last resort and our taxpayers can bail you out when you're in financial difficulty'?

There is, of course, another option – much advocated by more fundamentalist, but also sillier, Nats. That is for an independent Scotland to simply retain and use the pound without entering a currency union with the UK – so called 'sterlingisation'. However, such a system would mean that Scotland would have no central bank as a lender of last resort and would lose every last vestige of economic autonomy.

Advocates of this course point out that countries like Panama and El Salvador use the dollar in this way. How's that for a new level of ambition for an independent Scotland?

There is every sign that in all other parts of the present UK people are getting really hot under the collar about this behaviour on Mr Salmond's part. Although he's not normally averse to 'noising up' the English (although he's normally more caring of the Welsh and Northern Irish) this issue looks certain to rebound on the nationalists. Worst of all, in the eyes of many people in the rest of Britain, is the assumption, repeatedly voiced by Alex Salmond and Nicola Sturgeon, his deputy, that a sterling union in which an independent Scotland would participate would be in the 'best interests' of England, Wales and Northern Ireland, as well as of Scotland.

To this assertion, those beyond the Cheviots have loudly proclaimed: 'We shall decide what's best for us, not you, thank you very much. And if Scotland wants to be independent then it can bloody well go and do it but it will not be sharing OUR pound. Not a chance!'

Arguably, it is the one issue that has exercised British, and especially English, public opinion in the debate over Scottish independence more than any other. It has touched a raw nerve in a way nothing else has. It appears that the barefaced cheek of the Nats on the issue has been the last straw for the normally tolerant English. They have seen the SNP insist that they'll keep the Queen after independence and that they'll become a member of NATO, even though they'll kick 'Britain's' Trident nuclear deterrent out of Scotland. Both have caused an undercurrent of unhappiness amongst people elsewhere in the UK but essentially it appears that Salmond is effectively gambling on London blinking first, and ultimately failing to deny him the pound. But a long shot like that is no substitute for a proper economic policy.

# CONCLUSION

At the end of the day in the privacy and solitude of the polling booth, I am sure that as many people will be swayed by emotion as by practical considerations – such as tax and pensions. This is partly because there are conflicting and confusing messages out there that the ordinary voter may find it impossible to quantify one way or the other for themselves and their families. Professor Richard Finlay of Strathclyde University has summed this situation up quite neatly, I think, thus: 'It's NOT the economy, stupid'.

Too many people are hedging their bets and refusing to say how they'll vote because they claim there isn't enough information out there. This is rubbish. What people seem to want is their own personal P60, explaining exactly what their own circumstances would be like after independence. They are not going to get that. The information, in general, is all out there. Voters must simply decide who they choose to believe.

A number of major British companies, including Standard Life and RBS, have now warned about the possibly damaging effects of independence and the Governor of the Bank of England has said that the latter would probably have to move its headquarters to England. TSB has already done this. They won't be the last.

The many links that most people have with relatives and friends in the rest of the UK, in what is after all a mongrel nation, will, I believe, play a large part in deciding the referendum outcome.

And, essentially, it comes down to this. Of course Scotland could be an independent country. After all there are similar-sized and smaller countries already doing it but, after 300 years, why would we want to do it? There is absolutely no conclusive evidence that it will make anything better and it would make a lot of things much, much worse.